PURPLE GOLDFISH

SERVICE EDITION

THE 12 WAYS HOTELS, RESTAURANTS, AND
AIRLINES WIN THE RIGHT CUSTOMERS

STAN PHELPS

&

BROOKS BRIZ

Published by 9 INCH MARKETING, LLC
Cary, North Carolina

Copyeditor: Jennifer Phelps
Cover Designer: Evan Carroll

Ordering Information:
Special discounts are available on quantity purchases by corporations, associations, and others. For details, email: books@purplegoldfish.com.

First Edition

ISBN: 978-0-9849838-4-1
1. Business. 2. Marketing 3. Customer Experience 4. Word of Mouth

Printed and bound in the United States of America

*This book is dedicated to my beautiful wife, Jenn,
and our two boys, Thomas and James.
Their support and love made the
Purple Goldfish Project possible.*

—Stan Phelps

*This book is dedicated to God, you,
and everyone that helped us along the way.*

—Brooks Briz

ACKNOWLEDGEMENTS

Purple Goldfish is a crowdsourced book where people all over the world contributed examples that embodied the principles that we will set forth in Part I of this book. We would like to thank everyone who supported us and provided feedback or examples for this book, including, but certainly not limited to:

Triangle AMA, Jay Baer, Chad Blessed, Bruce Brizendine, Cafe Carolina, Evan Carroll, Ted Coiné, Saurabh Chawla, Udit Chaudry, Susan George, Phil Gerbyshak, Bryan Harris, Jessica Harris, Evan Hoffman, Shep Hyken, Kerry Johnston, Jeanne Jones, Jim Joseph, Denise Marshall, Sammie Marshall, Jennifer Phelps, Ted Rubin, David Rendall, Amber Sersen, Dee Ann Turner, Chris Zane, David Zendel, and countless others!

PRAISE FOR PURPLE GOLDFISH

"The concept of lagniappe is as old as the baker's dozen - and just as rare in business today! If you read just one book on customer experience all year, make it Stan Phelps and Brooks Briz's *Purple Goldfish: Service Edition*. From its pages you and your team will encounter countless examples of customer delight - well over the promised 1,001! If that isn't lagniappe, I don't know what is."

— TED COINÉ, CEO OF OPENFOR.BUSINESS, HOME OF THE EXTRAORDINARY INFLUENCER NETWORK AND AUTHOR OF *A WORLD GONE SOCIAL: HOW COMPANIES MUST ADAPT TO SURVIVE*

"I often remind myself what a wonderful opportunity it is to serve other people. In today's business landscape, we have no choice but to make a difference in the people's lives that we serve. When we commit to genuinely serving others; the stories that our guests tell about us will be the catalyst for our growth. *Purple Goldfish* will show you exactly how to do this."

— JOHN RIVERS, FOUNDER OF 4RIVERS SMOKEHOUSE AND BEST-SELLING AUTHOR OF *THE SOUTHERN COWBOY COOKBOOK*

"*Purple Goldfish: Service Edition* is the new benchmark for customer service and experience excellence. The single source for numerous concepts and innovations that can help build the foundation for a world class brand! I just hope my competition doesn't find this book."

— CHRIS ZANE, FOUNDER AND PRESIDENT OF ZANE'S CYCLES AND AUTHOR OF *REINVENTING THE WHEEL: THE SCIENCE OF CREATING LIFETIME CUSTOMERS*

CONTENTS

FOREWORD VIII

PROLOGUE TO THE SERVICE EDITION X

PREFACE XIV

WHAT IS A PURPLE GOLDFISH? 1

THE BIGGEST MYTH IN MARKETING 3

VALUE IS THE NEW BLACK 9

WHY PURPLE AND WHY A GOLDFISH? 15

A LITTLE SOMETHING EXTRA 25

POWERED BY GIFT ECONOMY PRINCIPLES 35

THE 5 INGREDIENTS OR R.U.L.E.S. OF A PURPLE GOLDFISH 45

FIRST INGREDIENT: RELEVANCY 47

SECOND INGREDIENT: UNEXPECTED 51

THIRD INGREDIENT: LIMITED 57

FOURTH INGREDIENT: EXPRESSION 63

FIFTH INGREDIENT: STICKY 67

12 TYPES OF PURPLE GOLDFISH 79

THE VALUE/MAINTENANCE MATRIX 81

#1 - THROW-INS 87

#2 - UNEXPECTED EXTRAS 103

#3 - SAMPLING 113

#4 - FIRST & LAST IMPRESSIONS 121

#5 - GUARANTEES 131

#6 - PAY IT FORWARD 137

#7 - FOLLOW-UP 143

#8 - ADDED SERVICE 153

#9 - WAITING 165

#10 - CONVENIENCE 173

#11 - SPECIAL NEEDS 179

#12 - HANDLING MISTAKES 195

LAGNIAPPE CATEGORY: TECHNOLOGY 203

TOP 10 KEY TAKEAWAYS 211

FOREWORD

BY DEE ANN TURNER

People ask how my employer has created a loyal following of fans. Just like any business, there are a multitude of reasons. When I consider all of the things that our franchisees and their employees excel at, I believe it all boils down to one thing that they do arguably better than anyone else in the world: they care about people, personally.

Close your eyes for a moment and ask your what comes to mind, what you see, and what you feel when you think of a remarkable fast food experience. I hope that you're currently envisioning smiling faces, courteous team members, a clean building, and delicious food. You might even hear a team member acknowledging a request of yours by saying, "It's my pleasure."

Many iconic brands are effective in eliciting positive thoughts and emotions from the guests they serve. Most of them are skilled in using their five senses to envision and then deliver a remarkable experience. The only possible way for us to compete in today's landscape is by truly making an impact in other people's lives by the work that we do.

Briz and Phelps have set the tone in *Purple Goldfish* for how guest expectations are changing in business. They offer staggering statistics about how traditional advertising has lost it value and instead they endorse genuine and friendly hospitality as a method to attract guests and keep them returning again and again. What this book also proposes is giving a little extra that either provide your customers more value or help maintain the relationship. The emphasis here is more on the retention of your customers rather than acquisition.

By crowdsourcing nearly all of the anecdotes in this book, the authors have found the best examples from around the world. However, think for a second about how these examples were discovered. Briz and Phelps asked people from all walks of life to come up with just one example of remarkable customer service in all of the service industries. As the authors point out, and you'll see throughout this work, the same names came up over and over again. What does that say about the opportunity that you have as a business leader to truly make an impact?

It is true that any company can choose greatness and add value to their customer's experiences. That's not to say that all of what is being proposed is without cost. There are investments to be made in labor scheduling, training and development and enhanced service delivery. Ultimately, guests become more loyal to businesses that provide the best service and it is more sustainable and economical to invest in providing great service rather than trying to compete on price, location, or product.

This book is a direct challenge and opportunity for you. After reading this book, you'll know definitively as to whether you want to do business as you always have or if you're going to take the necessary action to connect to the hearts and minds of consumers. If you make the right choice of differentiating by adding value to your customer's experience, the question ultimately becomes, "What's our Purple Goldfish?" I hope that you choose wisely!

Dee Ann Turner is the Vice President of Corporate Talent at Chick-fil-A and best-selling author of *It's My Pleasure: The Impact of Extraordinary Talent and a Compelling Culture*

PROLOGUE TO THE SERVICE EDITION

BY BROOKS BRIZ

In 2012, the original book, *What's Your Purple Goldfish? - How to Win Customers and Influence Word of Mouth*, was released. This happened shortly after the time when I walked away from my job at a Google subsidiary to fry chicken for free at a fast casual restaurant startup in remote South Carolina. For three and a half months, I provided pro bono consulting to the developing chain and worked in operations to learn the ropes of management (hourly restaurant jobs had helped me pay for college). In the interim, I slept on an old college couch wedged between a ping pong table and a mini fridge full of stale Miller Lite.

Most people would say that I had verifiably lost my mind, and most people would be right. All I knew is that the service industry had my heart and that I was meant to serve others through remarkable food, drink, and service. I came to realize that I needed to devote my life to the hospitality industry and it's what I continue to do today.

Flash forward a few years and I had become a full-fledged restaurant operator. One day, a manager at another one of our restaurants, Matt, told me that he had met Stan Phelps. Matt raved about Stan's business insights and offered to let me borrow his copy of *What's Your Purple Goldfish* that Stan had given him. I picked the book up and I immediately felt compelled to shoot Stan an email.

It was as if Stan had emptied out the contents of my brain and put them in a book as our ideals were strikingly similar. Shortly thereafter I started researching Stan's work and found that he had just published an article about our restaurant and, lo and behold, the "lagniappe of the day" was one of my video newsletters. I'm still waiting for Stan's apology for unauthorized use of my "amazing" creative work, but that's a topic for another day.

Stan and I met about a month later and found out quickly that we both believed that the best way to differentiate in a "sea of sameness" was through touching the hearts and minds of the people that you serve. I believe that people who are congruent in their beliefs and actions inevitably attract one another. That's why the two of us connecting came so naturally, and it quickly led us to foster a successful personal and professional relationship.

The reason why we rewrote the original work and created the "service" edition is because we both have a passion and deep commitment to these industries. We see a lot of service industry pros needlessly suffer when we believe that the answer to their diminishing returns is quite simple. Let me explain the background for the problem that I'm alluding to and what I believe the simple solution is.

Consider Friedman's theory which states that the sole purpose of business is to provide a return to shareholders. This is the basis from which KPIs and quarterly dividend returns come from. It makes sense and most of us accept this principle at face value. The problem with this philosophy is that there's never enough of a return and executives get caught in a perpetual quarterly return cycle. For better or worse, ROI and profits are what validate the efficacy of leadership in most businesses.

I'm sure you've witnessed this firsthand time and again where quarterly top-line sales and bottom-line efficiencies have to be established. In my estimation, most companies choose the quick and easy route to drive top-line sales by discounting their brand and give just to get. To establish bottom-line core competencies, they typically hack at the product, labor, and physical plant which all, in turn, diminish in quality and damage morale. At the end of the day, sales cure all challenges. You need a strategy to drive people in the door, ensure they're coming back, and ensure they tell others about you.

To drive traffic, your first inclination is probably to start dedicating your budget to advertising in order to reach the masses. However, consumer attention has never been more fragmented and the value of traditional advertising has decreased significantly. I say "value" because advertisers provide a service, but it's too expensive, does not correlate to top-line, and doesn't capture attention as they claim[1]. (Side note- Traditional ad companies, please feel free to keep charging outlandish prices and save up as much as you can because no one will be buying from you in 2025 if you continue down this path and refuse to evolve.)

Consumers now have millions of ways to spend their time and we're bold enough to think that our message is so special that people will drop whatever they're doing to pay attention to us? Do we believe that our customers put our businesses on some sort of pedestal and all clamor over the opportunity to share our newest promotion with their friends? It's a staggering thought, but perhaps we have to show the people that we currently, and will potentially, serve that we care about them first if we're ever to receive anything in return.

What Stan and I are proposing in the newest edition of *Purple Goldfish* is not easy. I would equate the principles to brushing your teeth.

---

1. http://www.hbs.edu/faculty/Publication%20Files/14-055_2ef21e7e-7529-4864-b0f0-c64e4169e17f.pdf

If you brush your teeth quickly and haphazardly every so often, then sure, you'll get the job partially done. Perhaps there are even some "quick fix" solutions that you can utilize such as mouthwash, white strips, and an annual cleaning. In short, everything looks great on the outside, but the foundation is crumbling. It's those who are willing to brush thoroughly, floss, and show dedication in their daily upkeep that will still have a beautiful set of teeth when they're 80 years old while your competition is soaking their dentures in cleansers (if they haven't already died of tooth decay).

Stan and I are asking you to consider the long-term. The only possible thing that we can do to stand apart is to intentionally touch the hearts and minds of the people that we serve on a daily basis. This book will show you proven strategies, ideas, and anecdotes that you can leverage and apply in your own business. At the end of the day, it's difficult to quantify the impact of genuinely serving others and creating a remarkable experience. However, what we're advocating is the willingness to try and adapt to today's business landscape and allocate the resources necessary. Be willing and able to fail, test, and continually improve. Your stakeholders are counting on you.

PREFACE

"In marketing, I've seen only one strategy that can't miss - and that is to market to your best customers first, your best prospects second, and the rest of the world last."

—John Romero

" Marketing has changed so rapidly...more in the past five years than in the past 500 years," Marketo chief marketing officer, Sanjay Dholakia, recently told VentureBeat. Dholakia went on to say, "We're entering a golden age of marketing." In our estimation, Dholakia is stating that the power has shifted. The consumer has a bigger voice and traditional "tell and sell" marketing has taken it in the shorts.

One of the more popular ways of framing this debate is that consumers have transitioned from being the "hunted" and have now become the "hunters." According to consultant Gordon Burrell, "The deer now have guns...get into the ammunition business." In other words, the personal media revolution has forever altered the relationship between companies and consumers which means that we all need to pay attention and figure out how to adapt.

Here are the top ten ways that marketing is changing and how it impacts the service industries:

> 10. "Retention" is becoming the new acquisition in marketing. It now costs up to ten times the amount of money to acquire a new customer than it does to keep a current one.[1]

> 9. 90% of customers identify word of mouth as the best, most reliable, and trustworthy source for ideas and information on products or services.[2]

> 8. Consumers are not paying attention to traditional media. Nearly 84% of consumers say that they fast

1. http://bit.ly/ForbesRetention
2. http://www.businessweek.com/debateroom/archives/2011/12/word_of_mouth_is_the_best_ad.html

forward through TV commercials or leave the room when commercials are on.[3]

7. Competition is steadily increasing, and there is always an alternative. More than 78% of consumers will abandon a brand because of a bad customer experience.[4]

6. Consumers may not know what they like, but they like what they know or what their network knows. According to McKinsey, 67 percent of all consumer decisions are primarily influenced by others.[5]

5. Interruption marketing has run amuck. In the 1970s, the average consumer was exposed to 500 to 2,000 messages per day. Today, consumers are approached with 3,000 to 5,000 messages per day. How do you expect to break through all of that noise?[6]

4. Love is a battlefield, for customers and marketing. Survey says: 94% of business leaders say customer experience is the new battlefield.[7] Pat Benatar could not be reached for comment.

3. Forget the water cooler. The online social landscape has become a game changer. According to author, Pete Blackshaw, "Today's satisfied customer tells three friends, an upset customer tells 3,000."[8]

3. http://blogs.wsj.com/cmo/2014/05/28/why-the-c3-v-c7-debate-in-tv-advertising-may-be-irrelevant

4. https://www.helpscout.net/75-customer-service-facts-quotes-statistics

5. http://bit.ly/McKinseyExperience

6. http://sjinsights.net/2014/09/29/new-research-sheds-light-on-daily-ad-exposures

7. http://www.infor.com/content/pitfalls/think-your-customers-are-having-great-experiences.pdf

8. http://bit.ly/AngryCustomersBlackshaw

2. Double the Pleasure in Marketing. Customers gained through word of mouth have up to two times the lifetime value than regular customers.[9] They also bring in up to twice the number of referrals.

1. Customer Experience Reigns Supreme. According to Gartner, "In 2016, 89% of companies expect to compete mostly on the basis of customer experience. Four years ago, this number was 36%."[10] Will you be part of the 11% that refuses to compete on customer experience?

It almost seems as though everything we've ever known about marketing has been thrown out the window. Now that we've identified the shifts in reaching our customers, the question becomes what we can do about it. We believe the solution lies in creating your Purple Goldfish. The rest of this book will delve into what a Purple Goldfish is, the opportunities currently available to help you differentiate in your industry, and dozens of real-world anecdotes to give you ideas for your future strategy.

9. http://www.bain.com/publications/articles/the-economics-of-loyalty.aspx
10. http://blogs.gartner.com/jake-sorofman/gartner-surveys-confirm-customer-experience-new-battlefield

PART I

WHAT IS A PURPLE GOLDFISH?

CHAPTER 1

THE BIGGEST MYTH
IN MARKETING

*"The search for meaningful distinction is central to the marketing effort.
If marketing is about anything, it is about achieving customer-getting
distinction by differentiating what you do and how you operate. All else
is derivative of that and only that."*

—Theodore Levitt

TALL TALES FROM NYC

A few summers ago, Stan was in New York City with a colleague at a trendy rooftop bar. One of those places where the special of the night is a Miller Lite bottle for $14. The tandem were waiting to meet a few people before heading over to a networking event, and Stan noticed an older gentleman sitting on his own for over 30 minutes. It was obvious that he was waiting for someone. Stan decided to strike up a conversation about waiting by offering his standard line, "Did you know that we spend 10% of our life waiting?"

The new acquaintance and Stan started talking about waiting, and Stan stressed the importance of being on time. As soon as Stan said this, the "waiting man" (as he is now known) shook his head in disagreement and said something that Stan will never forget, "There is no such thing as being on time. Being on time is a fallacy. You either are early or you are late. No one is ever on time. Being 'on time' is a myth."

This was a complete paradigm shift for Stan and he immediately starting thinking about how this principle applies to marketing and meeting customer expectations. Stan has always thought that the idea of meeting expectations was a surefire recipe for losing business. Merely meeting expectations almost always guarantees that you will fall short. It's similar to playing "prevent" defense in football. Prevent defense only prevents you from doing one thing... winning.

This new paradigm has only made it clearer for us. Meeting expectations is the biggest myth in marketing. Santa Claus, the Tooth Fairy, and "meeting expectations" all have something in common. Kids, cover your eyes and ears...they are all myths.

In business, you either fall below expectations or you exceed them. There is no middle ground. It bears repeating, "There is no such thing as meeting expectations." In a world where 60-80% of customers describe their customer satisfaction as satisfied or very satisfied before going on to defect to other brands, "meeting expectations" is no longer an option.

CHOOSE YOUR PATH WISELY

There are two paths that diverge in the corporate woods. Many companies take the wide first path and are happy with just meeting expectations. Others consciously take the narrower and tougher road deciding to go above and beyond to do more than reasonably expected.

Author Seth Godin wrote about under promising and over delivering in a post entitled, "Once in a Lifetime."[1] Seth touches on these two paths:

> This is perhaps the greatest marketing strategy struggle of our time: Should your product or service be very good, meet spec and be beyond reproach or...should it be a remarkable, memorable, over the top, a tell-your-friends event?

> The answer isn't obvious, and many organizations are really conflicted about this. Delta Airlines isn't trying to make your day. They're trying to get you from Atlanta to Salt Lake City, close to on time, less expensive than the other guy and hopefully without hassle. That's a win for them.

---

1. http://sethgodin.typepad.com/seths_blog/2010/02/once-in-a-lifetime.html

Most of the consumer businesses (restaurants, services, etc.) and virtually all of the business to business ventures I encounter, shoot for the first (meeting spec). They define spec and they work to achieve it. A few, from event organizers to investment advisors, work every single day to create over-the-top remarkable experiences. It's a lot of work, and it requires passion.

You can't be all things to all people. Your strategy defines which path you will take but it's important that you don't get caught in the mushy middle. It boils down to the simple issue of meeting expectations. If all you want to do is meet expectations, then you are setting yourself up to become a commodity. If you are not willing to differentiate yourself by creating valuable experiences or little touches that go "above and beyond" for your customer then you will languish in the sea of sameness. Choose your path wisely.

TO UNDER-DELIVER OR OVER-DELIVER?

In today's climate, you need to stand out by answering two important questions:

1. What makes you different?

2. Is that differentiator a signature element?

Creating small, unexpected extras can go a long way to increasing retention, promoting loyalty, and generating positive word of mouth. Investing your marketing budget in current customers is the lowest hanging fruit in marketing. Focusing solely on prospects in the purchase funnel and neglecting actual customer experience is a recipe for disaster.

SHAREHOLDERS VS. CUSTOMERS

Stan's friend, Jarvis Cromwell, of Reputation Garage, asked an interesting question, "Why are corporations in business?" He proposed that there are two sides of the argument:

1. Milton Friedman's theory that the sole purpose of a corporation is to drive shareholder value. Friedman said, "There is one and only one social responsibility of business, and that is to engage in activities designed to increase profits."[2]

2. The late American economist and professor at Harvard Business School, Theodore "Ted" Levitt, offered a different theory that states that companies are solely in the business of getting and keeping customers. Levitt said, "Not so long ago companies assumed the purpose of a business is to make money. But that has proved as vacuous as saying the purpose of life is to eat...The purpose of a business is to create and keep a customer."[3]

What comes first then: the customer or the bottom line? The last 100 years have seen corporations solely focused on the bottom line. The approach has been to win at all costs with little or no regard to external effects, collateral damage or customer experience. The problem is that only pursuing the bottom line often neglects the customer. This was outlined in an article from Harvard Business School by James Allen, Frederick Reichheld, and Barney Hamilton:[4]

Call it the dominance trap: The larger a company's market share, the greater the risk it will take its customers for granted. As the money flows in, manage-

2. http://www.colorado.edu/studentgroups/libertarians/issues/friedman-soc-resp-business.html

3. http://dwgreen.com/2015/06/the-purpose-of-a-business-is-to-get-and-keep-a-customer

4. http://hbswk.hbs.edu/archive/5075.html

ment begins confusing customer profitability with customer loyalty, never realizing that the most lucrative buyers may also be the angriest and most alienated. Worse, traditional market research may lead the firm to view customers as statistics. Managers can become so focused on the data that they stop hearing the real voices of their customers.

The entire premise of *Purple Goldfish* is that the customer must come first. Customer experience should be priority number one. It's essential that you stop focusing all of your energy on "the two in the bush" (i.e. your prospects) and start taking better care of "the one in your hand" (i.e. your current customers).

CHAPTER 2

VALUE IS THE NEW BLACK

"Price is what you pay. Value is what you get."

—Warren Buffett

GIVE ME VALUE OR GIVE ME DEATH

In challenging economic times, the business climate often forces both brands and consumers towards a "value" model. Plain and simple, consumers are expecting more value from you. According to the *Brand Keys Customer Loyalty Index*,[5] successful brands are those that stand out because consumers think of them as valuable. Please be aware that we are not advocating consumers as using the term "value" synonymously for "cheap." Brand Keys analyzed consumer values, needs, and expectations and offered the following trends:

1. **Value is the new black:** Consumer spending, even on sale items, will continue to be replaced by a "reason to buy" at all. This may spell trouble for brands with no authentic meaning, whether high-end or low.

2. **Brand differentiation is brand value:** The unique meaning of a brand will increase in importance as generic features continue to propagate in the brand landscape. Awareness as a meaningful market force has long been obsolete, and differentiation will be critical for sales and profitability.

3. **Consumer expectations are growing:** Brands are barely keeping up with consumer expectations now. Every single day consumers adopt and devour the latest technologies and innovations, and hunger for more. Smarter marketers will identify and capitalize on unmet expectations. Those brands that understand where the strongest expectations exist will be the brands that survive and prosper.

4. **It's not just buzz:** Conversations and community are increasingly important, and if consumers trust the community, they will extend trust to the brand. This means not just word of

---

5. http://brandkeys.com/portfolio/customer-loyalty-engagement-index

mouth, but the right word of mouth within the community. This has significant implications for the future of customer service.

5. **Consumers talk with each other before talking with brands:** Social networking and exchange of information outside of the brand space will increase. This – at least in theory – will mean more opportunities for brands to get involved in these spaces and meet customers where they are.

USING PARETO TO FLIP TRADITIONAL MARKETING

Vilfredo Federico Damaso Pareto was an Italian economist who made a famous observation in 1906. Pareto stated, "20% of the population in Italy owns 80% of the property."[6] The rule was popularized in the early 1940's by management consultant, Joseph Juran, and is now commonly referred to as the "80/20 principle."[7] The 80/20 principle states that 20% of your customers will account for 80% of your profitability and that 20% of your efforts will net 80% of your top-line results.

THE PHELPS 80/20 COROLLARY

If we subscribe to the principle that, "80% of your results are generated by 20% of your efforts," then Stan would like to respectfully put forth the Phelps Corollary, which states, "80% of your efforts will net you 20% of the results." Now all we have to do is figure out which efforts provide the optimal results that we're all looking to establish.

Traditional marketing (AKA "tell and sell" broadcast advertising) is ineffective. According to the late legendary retailer, Joseph Wana-

6. http://www.pragcap.com/the-pareto-principle-and-wealth-inequality

7. http://www.entrepreneur.com/article/229294

maker, "Half the money I spend on advertising is wasted...the problem is that I don't know which half."[8] We believe that a 50% return is an understatement, and therefore, we propose that for the vast majority of your marketing dollars spent on the traditional funnel (the 80%) now provide marginal results. In other words, you receive one dollar worth of return for every four that you spend given the Phelps 80/20 Corollary.

THE REVOLVING DOOR EFFECT

There is a huge flaw when focusing the majority of your marketing efforts on the traditional purchase funnel. This imperfection is what is known as, "The Revolving Door Effect." If the majority of your marketing is mainly focused on prospective customers, you may be able to add between 10% to 25% of new customers per year.

Most companies would say, "Sign me up right now for an increase of 10% - 25% of customers per year!" The problem is that most businesses also have huge problems with retention. Without focusing on current customers, it's not uncommon for businesses to lose 10 to 25% of their customer base in a given year. In fact, you might negate all of your gains and end up creating a revolving door by not taking care of your new and current customers.

The overwhelming traditional view of marketing is the process of acquiring prospective customers. 80-90% of marketing budgets are aimed towards getting consumers into the purchase funnel. We've become so preoccupied with generating awareness and interest that we tend to forget about our most important asset, our current customers.

We need to flip that ratio on traditional marketing. We need to heed Pareto's Law and determine the 20% of traditional marketing

---

8. http://www.wpp.com/annualreports/2013/what-we-think/why-its-time-to-say-goodbye-to-ikthtmisoaiw

we are doing that is generating the strongest ROI. Once you've earmarked that vital 20%, it's time to put the remaining 80% to work by putting the focus squarely on your current customers. By putting the focus on your current customers, you can generate the following three benefits:

1. Reduce attrition;

2. Increase satisfaction and loyalty, and;

3. Promote positive word of mouth.

THE SEA OF SAMENESS

This all begs the question, "How do you stand out in a sea of sameness?" What is your one signature differentiator in customer experience? Instead of being a "me too," what is the one special thing your company does that is superior and distinctive in the eyes of your customers?

For example, in *The Fish Philosophy*[9] corporate training series, the staff of the famous Pike Place Market in Seattle, WA, emphasize how they put customers first and differentiate by allowing their customers to throw and catch their fish. In one particular video, a manager at Pike Place Market says, "The second that you try to throw the fish like us, you've already lost." In essence, copying can only make you the best copycat, but it won't be your differentiating factor.

Again, what is that little something extra that is tangible, valuable and talkable? What do you hang your hat on? How do you stand out from your competition? Consider some of the most notable examples in the service-based industries:

---

9. http://www.fishphilosophy.com

- What is your warm chocolate chip cookie like DoubleTree?

- What is your "Bags Fly Free" value like Southwest Airlines?

- What are your free peanuts and bonus fries like Five Guys?

- What is your $2,000 daily employee allowance like Ritz-Carlton?

In other words, "What's your Purple Goldfish?"

CHAPTER 3

WHY PURPLE AND WHY A GOLDFISH?

"The thing that makes something remarkable isn't usually directly related to the original purpose of the product or service. It's the extra stuff, the stylish bonus, the design or the remarkable service or pricing that makes people talk about it and spread the word."

—Seth Godin

WHY A GOLDFISH?

Kimpton Hotels is the main inspiration for a goldfish. The boutique hotel chain understands the importance of doing the little extra for customers. At a Kimpton property, there is alway gourmet coffee for free in the lobby. Each hotel does a wine tasting in the afternoon. The chain is also super pet-friendly.

Our favorite of their extra amenities also happens to be Kimpton's signature offering. If you are staying at a Kimpton for a few days (and perhaps are getting a little lonely), Kimpton will give you a pet goldfish for your stay. They call the program, "Guppy Love." Introduced at the Hotel Monaco in 2001, the program has become a differentiating element that has garnered national attention.[10] The hotel offers guests the ability to adopt a temporary travel companion. According to Kimpton:

> The program is a fun extension of our pet-friendly nature as well as our emphasis on indulging the senses to heighten the travel experience, says Steve Pinetti, senior vice president of sales and marketing for Kimpton Hotels and Restaurants. Everything about Hotel Monaco appeals directly to the senses, and 'Guppy Love' offers one more unique way to relax, indulge and promote health of mind, body and spirit in our home-away-from-home atmosphere.

GOLDFISH ON THE BRAIN

We'll be the first ones to admit it; we are oddly preoccupied with goldfish. Mainly because the average common goldfish is between three to four inches, yet the largest goldfish in the world is almost

---

10. http://www.cnbc.com/id/47890272

six times that size at 19 inches. Allow us to repeat that...almost five times larger! Imagine walking down the street and bumping into someone that was three stories tall. That would certainly capture your attention and would be worth talking about, wouldn't it?

FACT

The current *Guinness Book of World Records* holder for the largest goldfish hails from The Netherlands at a whopping 19 inches (50 centimeters). To put that in perspective, that's about the size of the average domestic cat.

How can there be such a disparity between your common goldfish and their monster cousins? It turns out that the growth of the goldfish is directly determined by five factors. Part of our obsession is our firm belief that the growth of a product or service is almost exactly identical to that of a goldfish. It turns out that the growth of a goldfish (your products and services) is directly affected by five factors:

#1. SIZE OF THE ENVIRONMENT

Growth Factor: The size of the bowl or pond.

Rule of Thumb: Direct correlation. The larger the bowl or pond, the larger the goldfish can grow.

What is the bowl or the pond in business? It's the market for your product or service. The smaller the market, the lesser growth opportunity. The bigger the market, the greater potential for growth.

#2. NUMBER OF GOLDFISH

Growth Factor: The number of goldfish in the same bowl or pond.

Rule of Thumb: Inverse correlation. The more goldfish, the less growth opportunity.

Who are the other goldfish if you are in business? The other goldfish are your competitors. The more competition, the harder it is to grow in your market.

#3. THE QUALITY OF THE WATER

Growth Factor: The water clarity and the amount of nutrients in the water the goldfish is in.

Rule of Thumb: Direct correlation. The better the quality of the water in terms of clarity and nutrients, the more the goldfish will grow.

FACT

A malnourished goldfish in a crowded, cloudy environment may only grow to two inches (five centimeters).

The quality of the water in business is the economic environment. The clarity of the water is akin to consumer confidence. The nutrients in the water represent the ability to obtain capital to drive growth. Greater access to capital and strong consumer sentiment allow for growth.

#4. FIRST 120 DAYS OF LIFE

Growth Factor: The nourishment and treatment they receive as baby goldfish.

Rule of Thumb: Direct correlation. The lower the quality of the food, water, and treatment, the more the goldfish will be stunted for future growth.

FACT

Baby goldfish are tiny. They are called a fry, as in "small fry."

In business, the first 120 days of life is your time as a start-up. Or it might represent the first four months of launching a new product or service. How a business does in this critical time will be a factor in future growth potential.

#5. GENETIC MAKEUP

Growth Factor: The genetic makeup of the goldfish.

Rule of Thumb: Direct correlation. The poorer the genes or the less differentiated, the less the goldfish can grow.

The equivalent of genetic makeup in business is differentiation. The more differentiated the product or service is from the competition, the better the chance for growth.

Let's assume you have an existing product or service and have been in business for more than six months. Do you have any control over the market, your competition or the economy? No, no, and no. The only thing you have control over is the genetic makeup of your business. Specifically, you have control over how you differentiate your product or service through the experience that you provide. In goldfish terms, how do you stand out in a sea of sameness?

WHY PURPLE?

The reasons for choosing the color purple are two-fold:

#1. Mardi Gras. Lagniappe is a Creole word the means, "a little something extra." Purple is an ode to the birthplace of the word, New Orleans, and the colors of its most famous event, Mardi Gras.

The most commonly held story behind the original selection of the Mardi Gras colors originates from 1872 when the Grand Duke of Russia, Alexei Romanov, visited New Orleans. Legend has it that the Grand Duke came to New Orleans in pursuit of a British actress named Lydia Thompson. During his stay, Romanov was given the honor of selecting the official Mardi Gras colors by the Krewe of Rex. His selection of purple, green and gold would also later become the colors of the House of Romanov.

The 1892 "Rex Parade" theme first gave meaning to the official Mardi Gras colors. Inspired by New Orleans and its traditional colors, purple was symbolic of justice, green was symbolic of faith, and gold was symbolic of power. This is the reason why Stan chose these colors for the first three books in the Goldfish series.

#2. Ode to Seth Purple in marketing represents differentiation. Seth Godin established purple as the color of differentiation in his seminal book, *Purple Cow*, back in 2003. Seth outlines the why, what, and how of becoming remarkable.

Seth sets up the premise of the book with a story:

> When my family and I were driving through France a few years ago, we were enchanted by the hundreds of storybook cows grazing on picturesque pastures right next to the highway. For dozens of kilometers, we all gazed out the window, marveling about how beautiful everything was. Then, within twenty minutes, we

started ignoring the cows. The new cows were just like the old cows, and what was once amazing was now common. Worse than common. It was boring.

Seth went further and defined where marketing is heading by saying, "The old rule: Create safe, ordinary products and combine them with great marketing. The new rule: Create remarkable products that the right people seek out."

PURPLE BOVINE VS. PURPLE GOLDFISH

Think of a "Purple Cow" as your product. Your product needs to stand out and be remarkable. A Purple Goldfish, on the other hand, is the distinctive way that you deliver that purple cow and the extra value that you provide. It's difficult to make a product stand out by itself, but there is low hanging fruit in adding value to your offering.

The difficulty in Seth Godin's "Purple Cow" principle is that you need to bake that remarkability into the product. That is extremely difficult to accomplish. But what if you created a few Purple Goldfish instead? A goldfish is something a whole lot smaller than a cow and much easier to create. Can small "purple" things make a big difference? Absolutely.

Imagine if you asked that same friend for a recommendation and they started gushing about "Product X" because of signature experience. It could be the customer service they received that they were not expecting (think: Chick-fil-A), a feature that the company decided not to charge for (think: Southwest and "Bags Fly Free"), or a small "thank you" gift with your purchase (think: Five Guys Burgers).

TURNING A PURPLE GOLDFISH INTO STRATEGY

Let's compare an overall proposed "Purple Goldfish Strategy" to the critically acclaimed model in the book, *Blue Ocean Strategy*.[11] According to authors, Kim and Mauborgne:

> Blue Ocean Strategy is based on the simultaneous pursuit of differentiation and low cost. Its goal is not to out-perform competition in the existing industry, but to create new market space or a blue ocean, thereby making the competition irrelevant. The opposite of blue ocean is red ocean. Characterized by competition and a crowded space, red ocean is bloody water.

A MIDDLE GROUND

The Purple Goldfish Strategy advocates differentiation by adding value to the end consumers. This encompasses finding signature elements that help you stand out, improving customer experience, reducing attrition, and driving positive word of mouth. This makes the customer experience more important than ever, and there are three leading indicators.

First, the cost of customer acquisition continues to rise, making increasing retention the lowest hanging fruit in marketing. Second, consumers now have a stronger voice given the emergence of social technologies like blogs, Facebook, YouTube, Instagram, Snapchat, TripAdvisor, and Yelp. Finally, competing solely on price will "commoditize" your product or service faster than ever.

---

11. https://www.blueoceanstrategy.com

RED OCEAN STRATEGY	PURPLE GOLDFISH STRATEGY	BLUE OCEAN STRATEGY
Compete in existing market space	Compete in existing market space, but stand out by giving little unexpected extras (G.L.U.E.)	Create uncontested market space
Beat the competition	Differentiate yourself from the competition	Make the competition irrelevant
Exploit existing demand	Exploit current customer base to reduce attrition, drive loyalty, and promote word of mouth	Create and capture new demand
Make the value-cost trade-off	Break the transactional market economy mindset and add value to exceed expectations	Break the value-cost trade-off
Align the whole system of a company's activities with its stategic choice of differentiation or low cost	Align the whole system of a company's activities in pursuit of differentiation via added value	Align the whole system of a company's activities with its pursuit of differentiation and low cost

Purple Goldfish Strategy floating between the Red and Blue Ocean Strategies[12]

According to our good friend, Jay Baer, over at Convince and Convert, "You probably think you're pretty good at customer service. After all, 80% of companies say they deliver superior customer service, but only 8% of their customers agree."[13] What Jay is saying is that nobody believes that their interactions with their customers are lousy, and yet no one wants to face the fact that their "baby" might be "ugly." This conundrum reminded us of one of our favorite quotes, "Everyone wants to go to heaven… but nobody wants to pay the price."

---

12. Red Ocean Strategy and Blue Ocean Strategy Copyright 2010 Kim & Mauborgne

13. http://www.jaybaer.com/hug-your-haters

CHAPTER 4

A LITTLE SOMETHING EXTRA

"We picked up one excellent word—a word worth traveling to New Orleans to get; a nice limber, expressive, handy word—lagniappe"

—Mark Twain

A SIMPLE MARKETING CONCEPT

Is it possible to move the needle towards achieving differentiation while driving retention and stimulating word of mouth? What if your marketing execution was 100% targeted with zero waste and was given with a personalized touch? It sounds like a fantasy, but we promise you that it's not.

We believe the answer lies in focusing a greater percentage of your marketing budget on your current customers rather than your prospects. Put another way, allocating your attention to the "one in hand" rather than the "two in the bush" through a concept called, "lagniappe."

WHAT IS LAGNIAPPE?

Lagniappe is a Creole word meaning "the gift" or "to give more." The practice originated in Louisiana in the 1840s where a merchant would give a customer a little something extra at the time of their purchase. It is a signature personal touch by the business that creates goodwill and promotes word of mouth. According to Merriam-Webster:[14]

LAGNIAPPE: (lan'yəəp, lăn-yăp') *Chiefly Southern Louisiana & Mississippi*

1. A small gift presented by a store owner to a customer with their purchase.

2. An extra or unexpected gift or benefit. Also called boot.

Etymology: Creole < Fr la, the + Sp ñapa, lagniappe < Quechuan yapa

---

14. http://www.merriam-webster.com/dictionary/lagniappe

INTERESTING FACT

Napa comes from yapa, which means "additional gift" in the South American Indian language, Quechua, from the verb yapay "to give more."

ENTER SAMUEL LANGHORNE CLEMENS

Mark Twain was smitten with the concept of lagniappe. He wrote about the concept in his memoir, *Life on the Mississippi:*

> We picked up one excellent word–a word worth traveling to New Orleans to get; a nice limber, expressive, handy word– "lagniappe." They pronounce it lanny-yap. It is Spanish–so they said. We discovered it at the head of a column of odds and ends in the [Times] Picayune [newspaper] the first day; heard twenty people use it the second; inquired what it meant the third; adopted it and got facility in swinging it the fourth. It has a restricted meaning, but I think the people spread it out a little when they choose. It is the equivalent of the thirteenth roll in a baker's dozen. It is something thrown in, gratis, for good measure.
>
> The custom originated in the Spanish quarter of the city. When a child or a servant buys something in a shop–or even the mayor or the governor, for aught I know–he finishes the operation by saying– 'Give me something for lagniappe.' The shopman always responds; gives the child a bit of licorice- root, gives the servant a cheap cigar or a spool of thread, gives the governor–I don't know what he gives the governor; support, likely.

A lagniappe, i.e. Purple Goldfish, is any time a business purposely goes above and beyond to provide a little something extra. It's a marketing investment back into your customer base. It's that unexpected surprise that's thrown in for good measure to achieve product differentiation, drive retention, and promote word of mouth.

IS IT JUST A BAKER'S DOZEN?

Some people assert that lagniappe is merely the bakers dozen but it most certainly isn't. In order to understand a baker's dozen, we need to travel back to its origin in England. The concept dates back to the 13th century during the reign of Henry III.[15] During this time, there was a perceived need for regulations controlling quality, pricing, and checking weights to avoid fraudulent activity in the baking industry. The Assize (Statute) of Bread and Ale was instituted to regulate the price, weight, and quality of the bread and beer manufactured and sold in towns, villages, and hamlets.

Bakers who were found to have shortchanged customers could be subject to severe punishment such as losing a hand with an ax. To guard against the punishment, the baker would give 13 for the price of 12, to be certain of not being known as a cheat (and subsequently keep their hand). The irony is that the statute deals with weight and not the quantity. The merchants created the "baker's dozen" to change perception. They understood that one of the 13 could be lost, eaten, burnt, or ruined in some way, leaving the customer with the original legal dozen.

Flash forward to centuries later and a baker's dozen has now become expected. Nowadays when we walk into a bakery and buy a dozen bagels, we expect the thirteenth on the house. Therefore, the baker's dozen is not a lagniappe. However, if you provided a

---

15. http://mentalfloss.com/article/32259/why-bakers-dozen-13

fourteenth bagel as part of the dozen, then that would be a Purple Goldfish.

ACTS OF KINDNESS

You can also think of a lagniappe as an act of kindness. We have identified three "Acts of Kindness" to distinguish exactly what we mean:

1. **Random Act of Kindness** - "1.0" version. We've all seen this before. Good deeds or unexpected acts such as upgrading a passenger to first class on a flight or offering a free dessert for consumers. They are usually one-off, feel-good activities. A random act of kindness draws upon gift economy principles in that they are given with no expectation of immediate return except for potential PR value.

2. **Branded Act of Kindness** – Next level or "2.0." Here the item given is usually tied closely with the brand and its positioning. It's less random, more planned, and involves a series of events. This has the feel of a traditional marketing campaign, and many brands are moving in this direction. According to the former EVP/CMO of Coca-Cola, Joe Tripodi, "Coke is leaning more towards expressions than traditional impressions." In other words, fewer eyeballs and more emphasis on touches. What is an expression or a touch? It's a like on Facebook, a video on YouTube, sharing a photo of your product, a tweet on Twitter, and so forth.

3. **Lagniappe Act of Kindness** – "3.0" level acts are manifested through kindness and are embedded into the brand. Giving little unexpected extras (GLUE) as part of your product or service. This is rooted in the idea of added value to every single transaction. Not a one off or a campaign, but an everyday prac-

tice that's focused on customers of your brand. The beauty of creating this type of Purple Goldfish is that there is no waste. You are giving that little extra to your current customers and accounting for it.

1.0 RANDOM	2.0 BRANDED	3.0 LAGNIAPPE
Unpromoted	Promoted	Unexpected/expected
Untargeted	Prospect + Customers	Customer focused
One off	Campaign	Everyday
Opportunistic	Planned	Ingrained
Relevant to the recipient	Relevant to the brand	Relevant to the brand + recipient
In the field	Near point of purchase	At point of purchase
PR focused	PR + Brand	PR + Brand + CX + WOM

Branded Acts of Kindness: Evolving from tactic to campaign to brand differentiator

CONSIDER THE CURLY FRY

Stan's friend, Rick Liebling, shared his insight on lagniappe. Rick wrote about a particular (albeit inadvertent) lagniappe that he has witnessed time and time again:

> It's a fantastic concept that explains how brands can benefit by giving consumers just a little bit extra. As I was reading "My life," a blog by my friend Anastasia Wylie, she made reference, via a Jason Mraz song, to one of my all-time favorite lagniappes. Ever go to a fast food joint, order regular french fries, and get one curly fry in the bag? Man, I love that! It's such an incredibly small thing, it's an accident of location really (the regular fries are right next to the curly fries in the kitchen). But it makes you feel like you received something you weren't supposed to, that others didn't get, and that

you wouldn't necessarily have asked for ("Hey, could you throw one curly fry in there please?"), but once you get it, you are overjoyed. That's a lagniappe.

We love how Rick has summarized the feeling you get when you receive a lagniappe. The curly fry is that unexpected little extra that truly makes consumers feel special.

PLUSSING: THE ART OF EXCEEDING EXPECTATIONS

When talking about exceeding expectations, an entire book could be written about Walt Disney and the principles that make Disney a magical place. In fact, Pat Williams did just that and penned an incredible book called, *How to Be Like Walt: Capturing the Disney Magic Every Day of Your Life*.[16] The book talks about a concept Walt called "plussing":

> Normally, the word "plus" is a conjunction, but not in Walt's vocabulary. To Walt, "plus" was a verb—an action word— signifying the delivery of more than what his customers paid for or expected to receive.
>
> There are literally hundreds, if not thousands, of examples of Walt "plussing" his products. He constantly challenged his artists and Imagineers to see what was possible, and then take it a step further...and then a step beyond that. Why did he go to the trouble of making everything better when "good enough" would have sufficed? Because for Walt, nothing less than the best was acceptable when it bore his name and reputation, and he did whatever it took to give his guests more value than they expected to receive for their dollar.

16. http://www.amazon.com/How-Be-Like-Walt-Capturing/dp/0757302319

Perhaps one of the best examples of Walt's obsession for "plussing" comes from Disney historian Les Perkins' account of an incident that took place at Disneyland during the early years of the park. Walt had decided to hold a Christmas parade at the new park at a cost of $350,000. Walt's accountants approached him and besieged him to not spend money on an extravagant Christmas parade because the people would already be there. Nobody would complain, they reasoned, if they dispensed with the parade because nobody would be expecting it.

Walt's reply to his accountants is classic: "That's just the point," he said. "We should do the parade precisely because no one's expecting it. Our goal at Disneyland is to always give the people more than they expect. As long as we keep surprising them, they'll keep coming back. But if they ever stop coming, it'll cost us ten times that much to get them to come back."

HOW DO I CREATE LAGNIAPPE?

Now that you understand the importance of lagniappe, we'll leave you with three stories that perfectly exhibit how this theory can be applied in service-based operations:

The first story that represents a lagniappe is about a company founded by a social worker and a psychologist with a passion for good food and a commitment to healthy living. Without the capital to open a restaurant, Stacy Madison and Mark Andrus began serving healthy pita bread roll-up sandwiches in Boston's Financial District. Their lunch cart was extremely popular, and soon lines started to form around the block. To make waiting a bit more palatable, Stacy concocted a lagniappe for customers waiting in line.

Each night, Stacy and her team would bake the leftover pita bread and sprinkle the bread with various seasonings to create different types of flavored chips. The chips were a huge hit and soon "Stacy's Pita Chip Company" was born. Stacy's experienced rapid growth, doubling sales every year and ultimately led to a multimillion dollar acquisition by Frito Lay in 2005.

The second story is about a restaurant based on the premise of this book with the same namesake. The Louisiana Lagniappe restaurant chain in the southeastern United States is notorious for its upscale ambiance, waterfront dining, fresh ingredients, outstanding service, and commitment to serving the community. Everything that Louisiana Lagniappe does in regards to its building, service, food, and every component of their experience is intended to provide "just a little something extra." Perhaps that's why Louisiana Lagniappe locations are consistently ranked on TripAdvisor's "Top 10 restaurants" in every community that they serve and win the TripAdvisor "Award of Excellence" year after year. Arguably the most notorious extra that they provide comes in the form of complimentary beignets while you wait and during their popular brunch service. Coupled with one dollar mimosas, the value that guests receive from Louisiana Lagniappe is what sets the chain in a league of its own.

The final story comes to us from Panera Bread. Gail Cook of Wilton, New Hampshire, posted a Facebook status update on Panera Bread's business page that read:

> My grandmother is passing soon with cancer. I visited her the other day, and she was telling me about how she really wanted soup, but not hospital soup because she said it tasted "awful" and she went on about how she really would like some clam chowder from Panera. Unfortunately, Panera only sells clam chowder on Friday. I called the manager Sue and told them the situa-

tion. I wasn't looking for anything special just a bowl of clam chowder. Without hesitation, she said absolutely she would make her some clam chowder. When I went to pick it up, they wound up giving me a box of cookies as well. It's not that big of a deal to most, but to my grandma, it meant a lot. I really want to thank Sue and the rest of the staff from Panera in Nashua, NH, just for making my grandmother happy. Thank you so much!

The Panera story was "liked" over 800,000 times and received nearly 35,000 comments on Facebook alone and has been covered in multiple major news outlets. As you can see, one little lagniappe garnered the type of coverage, attention, and engagement that most brands can only dream of. This is why we believe that doing the little things truly make the biggest difference.

CHAPTER 5

POWERED BY GIFT ECONOMY PRINCIPLES

"There are two types of economies. In a commodity (or exchange) economy, status is accorded to those who have the most. In a gift economy, status is accorded to those who give the most to others."

—Lewis Hyde

EXPLORING THE IDEAS OF SURPLUS & STATUS

W e're fascinated by the concept of a "gift economy" and how it relates to providing a Purple Goldfish. If you've never heard of the gift economy, it's a social science principle that states valuable goods and services are regularly given without explicit agreement for immediate or future rewards. In a perfect world, simultaneous or recurring giving serves to circulate and redistribute valuables within a society. Put another way; it's the principle of reciprocity in motion.

A gift economy is the opposite of a market economy. In a market economy, there is an exact exchange of values (quid pro quo). It is our theory that there is a hybrid called the lagniappe economy that can sit between the gift and market economies.

HOW CAN A LAGNIAPPE LIVE IN THESE ECONOMIES?

Here is a great analysis from a post by Kevin von Duuglass-Ittu on gift economies:

This does not mean that the Gift Economy...and the Market Economy of business are incompatible, not in the least. In fact, many, if not most, of our business exchanges are grounded in gift-based relationships whose "gift" nature we simply are unconscious of and just assume. If you develop a keen eye for the gift-giving environment, and think about all the things that gift-giving in those environments signal: 1. A surplus others want to attach themselves to, 2. A magnanimous respect for the relationship beyond all else, 3. A debt structure that is positive.

Let's examine each of the three environments through the lens of a lagniappe economy:

1. **Surplus** – The idea of surplus is grounded in giving extra or creating an inequality. Lagniappe is the practice by the business of throwing in little extras at the time of purchase.

2. **Respect** – The gift or little extra is about the respect for the relationship. It becomes a beacon, a sign that shows you care. It's a physical sign of goodwill and customer appreciation.

3. **Positive** – A debt structure that is positive. This speaks to exceeding expectations by giving extra. The idea of an equal exchange (market exchange) is a myth in marketing. You either exceed or fall short of customer expectations. Providing that extra value provides an inequality that is positive. The positive effect leads to a sort of indebtedness or reciprocity on behalf of the customer.

THE BENEFIT OF A SURPLUS IS STATUS

As a business, why would you want to incorporate gift economy principles into your market exchanges? We believe that there are three distinct reasons and corresponding benefits of the status gained through providing a lagniappe:

1. **Positioning** – Stand out from your competition. If everyone is providing "x," the fact that you provide "x + y" (gift) then differentiates your offering. Less than 30 percent of consumers buy on price. You want to tap into the 70+ percent who are looking for value and a strong customer experience. **Benefit: Differentiation**

2. **Loyalty** – Giving the little extra (gift) enhances the customer experience. It creates a bond between the business and the customer. The benefits of that bond result in increased loyalty and ultimately patronage as a form of repayment. **Benefit: Retention**

3. **Reciprocity** – Part of giving extra is to create goodwill (inequality). That inequality is repaid by positive word of mouth or digital word of mouse. The best form of marketing is via positive word of mouth. By giving a signature extra (gift), you provide something for your customers to talk, tweet, blog, Yelp or post to Facebook about. **Benefit: Referrals**

THE POWER OF A CHOCOLATE CHIP COOKIE

Stan recently had a quick business lunch at the Port Chester Coach Diner in Port Chester, New York. Upon paying at the counter, Stan noticed a bowl of miniature chocolate chip cookies. Stan asked his colleague, Tim Heath, to recap the experience and encountering the cookies:

> We were pleased with the rapid and attentive service and quality of food. I walked away from the table content; but you guessed it, I was seeking a little some-

thing more to satisfy my appetite. Much to our pleasure, there was a container of complimentary small chocolate chip cookies next to the cash register. Stan and I looked at each other simultaneously with a smile. We both ate two free cookies, and we shared our pleasure with the owner who was observing our enthusiastic response to his offering. A pleasant ending to a fine lunch. I look forward to my next meal at the Port Chester Coach Diner.

The chocolate chip cookie was a thread throughout the original Purple Goldfish Project where Stan set out to collect 1,001 examples. DoubleTree, and their signature chocolate chip cookie, was cited so many times that DoubleTree became the first brand inducted into the Purple Goldfish Hall of Fame. The hotel has built a reputation on a unique treat that keeps leisure and business travelers coming back for more: its legendary chocolate chip cookie presented to each guest at check-in.

Here are a few fun facts about the legendary cookie:

- DoubleTree gives out approximately 60,000 chocolate chip cookies each day. That's more than twenty million each year!

- DoubleTree began giving out chocolate chip cookies in the early 1980s, when many hotels across the country used them as treats for VIPs.

- In 1995, DoubleTree enlisted the services of Nashville-based, Christie Cookie Company, to hold the brand's secret recipe, which ensures that the same, delicious cookie is delivered consistently at every DoubleTree property.

- Every DoubleTree chocolate chip cookie is baked fresh daily at each hotel.

- Each cookie weighs more than two ounces and has an average of 20 chocolate chips.

- The Christie Cookie Company uses more than 580,000 pounds of chocolate chips each year for DoubleTree's cookies.

- To date, more than 300,000,000 cookies have been served to delighted guests and customers.

- More than one million chocolate chip cookies have been donated by DoubleTree hotels to celebrate and thank deserving members of the community from doctors and nurses to police and firefighters, as well as non-profit groups such as orphanages, food banks, and homeless shelters.[17]

WHAT'S SO SPECIAL ABOUT THE COOKIE?

DoubleTree offers an explanation right on the brown paper bag the cookie comes in. "Why a cookie?" the headline asks. "Cookies are warm, personal and inviting, much like our hotels and the staff here that serves you." In a recent *New York Times* article, a Vivaldi Partners executive, Erich Joachimsthaler, said:

> When consumers don't know how to judge the benefits or the differentiation of a product — I don't know the difference between Midwest and JetBlue and United — then a meaningless attribute like cookies can create meaningful differentiation...The giveaway creates buzz, it creates differentiation, it increases a purchase decision.

We don't necessarily agree with the word "meaningless," especially if that little extra is a signature element. We subscribe to the phi-

---

17. http://www.doubletreecookies.com/the_cookie_history

losophy that Malcolm Gladwell offered in *The Tipping Point,* "The little things can make the biggest difference."[18] The chocolate chip cookie is not just a chocolate chip cookie. It's much more than that.

GREETINGS AND GIFTING AS A ONE - TWO PUNCH

A recent study in the *International Journal of Marketing Studies*[19] has revealed that giving a gift before the purchase could increase consumer spending by over 40 percent. Here is a synopsis of the article by authors, Hershey H. Friedman and Ahmed Rahman:

> An experiment was conducted in a restaurant to determine the effects of a small gift upon entry and greeting customers with a thank you for their patronage. Two types of gifts were used: a cup of yogurt and an inexpensive key chain. The authors found that providing a gift upon entry into a store had an impact on how much was spent, on the performance rating, and on how strongly the establishment would be recommended. This study did not find any differences between gifts: a gift of a cup of yogurt had the same impact as a key chain. The difference in amount spent between the group that was not greeted or given a gift ($7.11) and the group that was greeted and given a cup of yogurt ($10.41) was 46.4% higher, a considerable amount.

The article discusses the underlying principle of reciprocity, the power of surprise, and the importance of giving without an implicit expectation of return. The conclusions are very interesting:

---

18. http://gladwell.com/the-tipping-point
19. http://www.onefiftynine.com/assets/File/Blog%20Downloads/Customer%20Loyalty%20Research.pdf

This study demonstrates that there is value in greeting customers who enter a store. Customers who are not greeted will spend considerably less, will rate the store lower on performance, and will also be less likely to recommend the establishment. Providing a small gift upon entry into a store will have an impact on how much is spent, on the performance rating, and on how strongly the establishment will be recommended.

The value of a satisfied customer to a business is immense. One study showed that customers who are totally satisfied contribute 17 times more sales to a firm than customers who are somewhat dissatisfied and 2.6 times as many sales as customers who are somewhat satisfied. If all it takes to improve attitudes of customers is an appreciatory comment and an occasional gift, then organizations should use this approach as part of their marketing communications strategies.

FROM YOGURT TO PEANUTS

Another member of the Purple Goldfish "Hall of Fame" is Five Guys Burgers and Fries. Founder, Jerry Murrell, and his eponymous five sons represent the principles of a lagniappe. For background, Matt and Jim travel the country visiting stores, Chad oversees training, Ben selects the franchisees, and Tyler runs the bakery.

Added value is baked into the model at Five Guys:

- Free peanuts when you walk through the door;

- 15 free toppings for your hamburger or hot dog;

- An extra handful or two of "bonus" fries;

- Free refills for your soda or ice tea, and;

- The building is free of logos and excess décor.

The free peanuts that you can shell are our favorite. While you wait for your order to be prepared, there is a mountain of peanuts just inside the front door to munch on. Free peanuts have become the trademark "thing" that Five Guys is known for. You'll often see over fifty bags, 50 pounds apiece, waiting to be opened and devoured next to the door. Overall, it's a cool thing: order your cheeseburger and scarf down a handful of salty, ballpark-style, still-in-the-shell peanuts.

By our rough calculations, Five Guys gives away over five million pounds of peanuts per year. Do little things make a big difference? For a company that does little to no advertising, we would certainly say so. The mantra from Jerry Murrell is, "We figure that our best salesman is our customer. Treat that person right, he'll walk out the door and sell for you. From the beginning, I wanted people to know that we put all our money into the food."[20]

---

20. http://www.inc.com/magazine/20100401/jerry-murrell-five-guys-burgers-and-fries.html

PART II

THE 5 INGREDIENTS OR R.U.L.E.S. OF A PURPLE GOLDFISH

CHAPTER 6

FIRST INGREDIENT: RELEVANCY

"Existence is no more than the precarious attainment of relevance in an intensely mobile flux of past, present, and future."

—Susan Sontag

MAKING LAGNIAPPE IS LIKE JAMBALAYA

Have you ever made jambalaya from scratch? It's a bunch of different ingredients all thrown in together where the chef takes a look at what's lying around in the kitchen and throws it all into a pot. Let your concoction stew with some spices thrown in and...voilà! You have yourself a jambalaya or a Purple Goldfish, in this case. Here are the five main ingredients of our jambalaya (or if you are an acronym fan as we are) the R.U.L.E.S.:

Relevant – The item or benefit should be of value to the recipient.

Unexpected – The extra benefit or gift should be a surprise. It is something thrown in for good measure.

Limited – If it's a small token or gift, it has to be rare, hard to find or unique to your business.

Expression – Many times it comes down to the gesture. It becomes more about "how" it is given, as opposed to "what" is given.

Sticky – Is it memorable enough that the person will want to share their experience by telling a friend or everyone that they know?

KEEPING IT RELEVANT

The first rule and probably the most important ingredient for a Purple Goldfish is relevancy. If it's just a throw-in or SWAG (stuff we all get), then the gift is probably not that relevant. It needs to be a gift that is actually valued by your customer. Let's look at a few examples that are truly relevant in their offerings.

ENJOY IT NOW AND LATER

Georgia Brown's, an iconic restaurant in Washington, DC, is famous for a lot of different aspects. Perhaps most notably is their exquisite brunch offering complete with live jazz music. What many people did not know, but are now coming to expect, is that Georgia Brown's offers a free entree to go.

According to our friend, Keonna Yates, "Georgia Brown's restaurant in DC has an amazing brunch. If you go there for brunch, you also get a dinner entree for free to go. It's the perfect size to eat later in the evening." Georgia Brown's also offers little unadvertised extras such as free valet parking which is quite an anomaly in Washington, DC.

The fact that the restaurant can get guests in and out efficiently is a bonus in and of itself. Not only do diners get the unique experience of omelets made to order served alongside live music but they also get to remember their visit later on that day. That's what we call relevant added value!

GET TWO CONES FOR THE ROAD

How about making a cone in the comfort of your home? Here is what Molly Holtman shared about Toy Boat:

> Toy Boat, a great dessert shop on Clement Street in San Francisco, throws in two complimentary ice cream cones (cake or sugar, your choice) when you purchase a pint of ice cream. It's kind of fun to eat ice cream in a cone at home. Plus, their rocky road and pumpkin ice cream are both fantastic.

This a thoughtful and simple complimentary touch from Toy Boat... dare we say, sweet genius.

MORE THAN REWARD POINTS

Choice Hotels based out of Rockville, MD, features a rewards program that has a few interesting twists. Not only do new members receive rewards for joining the program such as Amazon gift cards, airline miles, and additional points, but Choice constantly goes above and beyond to provide unique gifts that make stays more comfortable. One example is the "Cambria welcome gift" which includes a free beverage at the bar when guests arrive. Choice also allows its guests to gift their points to others so that their network can enjoy the same luxurious amenities and accommodations.

MINIBAR PRICES THAT DON'T INCLUDE YOUR FIRSTBORN

One of the negative stigmas associated with hotels are the "convenient" minibars in rooms that offer a variety of snacks, drinks, and adult beverages. You're welcome to indulge in the hedonistic paradise and typically love life until you receive the bill and realize that you have to take out a second mortgage. Kimpton Hotels (the very same as the "Guppy Love" program) have instituted a rewards program called "Kimpton Karma" which aims to differentiate their offering from the industry-wide practice.

Kimpton Karma has four levels of membership and all of the levels feature a "Raid the Minibar" offer that allows guests to take a snack or refreshment or two from their room's minibar free of charge. Kimpton's website explains the program, "Who doesn't love a free drink or snack? Raid the Bar provides one $10 credit ($15 in NYC) to spend at either our restaurant bar or the in-room honor bar during each of your eligible stays."[21]

---

21. https://www.kimptonhotels.com/karma-rewards/overview

CHAPTER 7

SECOND INGREDIENT: UNEXPECTED

"So what exactly is 'surprise and delight?'
It's when you give your customer something - that little gift
or 'extra mile' - that they didn't expect.
Surprise and delight is that small benevolent act that
shows that you put the customer first, and that
you're willing to make their experience special."

—Marc Schiller

WHAT THE HECK IS A SCHEMA?

S teve Knox of Tremor, a P&G agency, took Stan to school recently. Steve wrote an enlightened post in Ad Age[22] entitled, "Why Effective Word of Mouth Disrupts Schemas." The article explains how to leverage cognitive disruption to drive word of mouth. By doing something unexpected, people feel compelled or even "forced" to talk about the experience.

First off, let us admit that we had no clue what a "schema" was. Here is our interpretation of the word. It turns out that our brain remains typically in a static state. It relies on developing cognitive schemas to figure out how the world works. It recognizes patterns and adapts behavior accordingly. Your brain doesn't want to have to think.

For example, every day you get into the car, and you know instinctively to drive on the right side of the road. Fast forward and you're on a trip to the UK or Australia. The first time you drive on the left side, it throws you for a loop. It's disruptive to your normal driving schema, and it forces the brain to think which thereby elicits discussion (i.e. word of mouth).

Steve also provided some great examples in his article. Our favorite example was for a new Secret deodorant that P&G was launching which featured a deodorant that utilized a moisture activated ingredient which kicked in when you sweat. The brand understood that this could be positioned against a traditional schema which was understood by their focus groups that stated, "the more you work out, the more you sweat, and the worse that you smell." Ultimately, the tagline for the brand became, "The More You Move, the Better You Smell." A staggering 51,000 consumers posted comments on P&G's website about the product.

---

22. http://adage.com/article/cmo-strategy/marketing-effective-word-mouth-disrupts-schemas/141734/

Stan started thinking how this idea of disruption applies to the concept of a lagniappe. The second ingredient in the lagniappe R.U.L.E.S. is the concept of being "unexpected." It's that little something that's an unexpected extra at the time of purchase. It's the unexpected surprise and delight that triggers disruption of our schemas.

Let's face it...most companies fail to deliver an exceptional customer experience. It's only when a brand does anything to go above and beyond do we get shocked. And what happens when we receive that unexpected lagniappe act of kindness? We tell our friends, we tweet it, and we post to Facebook about it. Those are the only types of positive experiences that are amplified.

ANNIVERSARIES HAVE NEVER BEEN SWEETER

The Black + Blue restaurant in Vancouver, British Columbia, is famous for a lot of aspects but their commitment to making special occasions worth remembering is how they help set themselves apart. Black + Blue likes to allow its exemplary service and unexpected gifts fly under the radar as these aspects are not something that they advertise. According to one guest on TripAdvisor:

> We went to celebrate our 10th wedding anniversary, and our waiter was, "Brandon." The quality and attention that Brandon gave us was the best we've ever had and also the food was amazing. He made our special day one that we'll remember for the rest of our lives. He gave us complimentary champagne and dessert, which were delicious. I will recommend this place for special occasions as it's not cheap, but it'll be worth every penny.

AN EXTRA ACKNOWLEDGEMENT

Jack Monson recently shared this story from a business trip to Minneapolis, Minnesota:

> A few years ago, I was traveling to the Twin Cities often and stayed several times at the same Courtyard By Marriott in the suburb of Eden Prairie since it was close to two clients' respective headquarters. By the third trip in a few weeks' time, I had a nice surprise waiting for me. I walked in after a cold and delayed trip from Chicago to see a big sign in the lobby saying, "Welcome, Jack Monson." The manager informed me that I was their guest of the week (or whatever the title was) and gave me a card for free breakfast in the morning. Not a huge thing, but guess where I continued to stay every time I had to travel to Minneapolis over the next year.

KLM DOES A LITTLE EXTRA FOR FANS

Leaving something behind on a plane or in the airport can be a major drag. That's why Dutch airline, KLM, goes above and beyond to offer a "lost and found" service. According to KLM:

> A dedicated Lost & Found team is now on a mission to return items, found by cabin crew on board or by KLM airport staff, as soon as possible to their legitimate owners. Every week, KLM receives 40,000 questions via social media. One of the most asked questions is about getting lost items back. This inspired us to set up a dedicated KLM Lost & Found team that uses all available information like seat number, phone numbers and public social media details to reunite passengers with their belongings.

Most passengers do not know about the program so imagine their delight when they receive their lost item and find out that KLM actively sought out the missing luggage to return it to them. In fact, KLM went on to create a branded act of kindness by creating a video that featured a floppy-eared beagle named "Sherlock" that returned items to KLM's passengers. Though the video might have been staged and deemed a publicity stunt by some, it drove home their differentiator and racked up nearly 22 million YouTube views as of early 2016.[23]

RITZ SETS THE PRECEDENT

The Ritz-Carlton hotel chain is notorious for going above and beyond to service its guests. What's unparalleled is how much the hotel gives and how consistently they do so. Consider this example from the Ritz-Carlton in Orlando, FL, that we found on TripAdvisor, "I just mentioned that it was my wife's birthday then suddenly there was a complimentary two glasses of champagne with a nice birthday dessert platter. It was a very nice gesture. And it didn't stop there; my wife was given a small teddy bear toy with a sweet birthday card note."

To receive perhaps a dessert or a glass of champagne may have come to be expected but Ritz went above and beyond to provide both items, an additional gift, and a heartfelt birthday card. Talk about exceeding expectations. Here's another unexpected gift that another visitor of the Ritz-Carlton in Cancun, Mexico, from TripAdvisor:

> Room service was excellent. The housekeeping staff put my loose jewelry in a pouch to presumably prevent me from dropping or losing an earring; they noticed my husband put a towel down near the toilet (where the floor was cold for his bare feet) and the following

23. http://www.cnn.com/2014/09/24/travel/klm-dog

afternoon, an additional bath mat magically appeared in place of the towel. The beach servers all greeted us by name and remembered our preferences. Complimentary popsicles, beverages, aloe, and ice cold towels were regularly circulated for guests in the sun.

It's the little unexpected extras that differentiate an ordinary experience from the ones that are deemed extraordinary. It certainly doesn't hurt that the Ritz received a glowing five-star review and a guest that will recommend the resort to everyone that he knows (as per his review).

AN EXTRA DONUT ON THE HOUSE

According to reader, Graham Bargeron, "Faith, Coffee, Sweets is a family owned coffee shop in Harrisburg, NC. Home of the Maple Bacon donut, all donuts are made in-house. UNCC [The University of North Carolina at Charlotte] students get two free donuts with the purchase of any sized coffee. Most students don't even know about the donuts and are pleasantly surprised."

One donut could easily be expected as a special for college students. However, adding the additional product is what makes this unexpected extra stand alone. Remember when we said that the additional donut would merely qualify as the "Baker's Dozen" but that two extra would be a Purple Goldfish? Here's the case in point.

CHAPTER 8

THIRD INGREDIENT: LIMITED

"America has believed that in differentiation, not in uniformity, lies the path of progress. It acted on this belief; it has advanced human happiness, and it has prospered."

—Louis Brandeis

SIGNATURE TOUCH

The third of the R.U.L.E.S. is the concept of being "limited." What does limited mean? If it's a small token or extra, it means selecting something unique to your business. Ideally, you want it to be signature to your brand. Something rare, different or just plain hard to find elsewhere. A limited extra helps you differentiate your offering(s) while providing insurance against being copied by competitors.

A BUFFET AND AN AFTER DINNER APPLE

The Angus Barn of Raleigh, NC, is consistently listed as a top independent restaurant in the United States and has won more than 200 dining awards. The commitment to creating the ultimate guest experience is second to none, and no one can copy what the Angus Barn has created. According to our good friend, Jon Rowe:

> If I take my family here, then we'll typically dine in the main dining room but if I'm with clients or taking someone new to Angus Barn then I prefer to go upstairs to The Wild Turkey Lounge to eat. It's very warm, cozy, and much more comfortable (it's almost like being in your rich uncle's living room). For a limited time during the evening, the Angus Barn sets up a station full of wonderful crackers and cheese, celery, olives, and so forth, for snacking on while you are waiting for your meal.
>
> They have several cozy areas you can sit in to wait for your table if you don't have a reservation (sometimes the wait is well over an hour). You can also go upstairs to the Lounge to get a drink (featuring more delicious crackers and cheese) while you wait. It's a little pricey but is a great place for those special occasions. For

anyone that hasn't been there, it really does look like a barn inside and don't forget to grab a couple of free apples from the baskets on your way out!

The complimentary crackers and cheese buffet and "after meal" apples are brilliant. Both of these features score high on the five ingredients/rules of a perfect lagniappe. Let's look at this example in more detail:

Relevant – All of the gifts are given to enhance the appetite of diners and build goodwill.

Unexpected – The buffet tables seemingly appear out of nowhere, and extras are freely shared.

Limited – The complimentary "snack" tables are only available during certain hours.

Expressive – The apple baskets and buffet tables are joyfully restocked by the staff. You would think that they would be apprehensive about guests taking advantage of the free offerings, but nothing could be further from the truth.

Sticky – Anyone that has ever been to Angus Barn feels compelled to tell others about the experience. Go there and you'll see what we're talking about!

DONUT HOLES AND MILK DUDS

There are multiple reasons why native Chicagoans and tourists alike consider Lou Mitchell's a "must visit." From the donut holes and the milk duds while you wait to the double-yolk eggs that make every dish even more sinfully indulgent, Lou's knows how to do breakfast. Located in the South Loop, the restaurant has been a Chicago institution since 1923. Decades later, they're still dishing out thick French toast, enormous platters of pancakes, fresh-baked pastries, and of course, those famous skillets. The extras are just as delectable. Lou's boasts pure maple syrup, fresh-squeezed orange juice, and slabs of toast served with every omelet.

Be prepared to make some new friends — chances are good you'll be seated next to strangers at one of the lengthy tables. Even if you don't bond with fellow diners, the perpetually friendly smiles from the Lou Mitchell's team — and free Milk Duds for the ladies — guarantee that you'll want to return soon.

FOUR SEASONS PACKS A CHOP

A good friend, Doug Pirnie, shared his experience of staying at the Four Seasons and receiving their signature Purple Goldfish when checking out. According to Doug, "At the end of my stay at the Four Seasons in Singapore, they gave me my own personal 'chop' – a stamp with my insignia on it. Apparently it is a Chinese tradition for all personal documents to be stamped."

The hand stamp, especially for a Westerner, is something rare and unique. The addition of personalization on the stamp by the hotel makes it special. Two thumbs up for the staff at the Four Seasons who leveraged Chinese heritage to give a remarkable gift with the chop!

GUATEMALAN WORRY DOLLS

Besito means "little kiss" in Spanish. It's also the name of an authentic Mexican restaurant based in Roslyn, New York. Stan's friend, Lilliam Villafane De Giacomo, speaks ad nauseam about the amazing food but pays special attention to two added value items. At the end of the meal the restaurant hands out wrapped churros and little worry dolls.

A recent *New York Times* review mentions the churros and worry dolls:

> The best dessert was the churros given gratis to every table. The warm, long spirals of fried dough rolled in cinnamon sugar were delivered in a white paper bag. Along with them, we were given tiny worry dolls to be put under our pillows to take away worries. My only worry was the amount of delicious food I'd just eaten.

We could fill the rest of this book up with the litany of positive reviews about the worry dolls and the complimentary churros but here is another one of our favorite reviews from Zomato:

> A fresh dish of chunky guacamole is created at your table side from perfectly ripened fruits in a molcajete, the authentic Mexican basalt lava version of a mortar and pestle. It was near perfect for my tastes. Even at twelve bucks a pop we occasionally have two bowls. Their beef enchilada, huevos rancheros and chicken enchilada in creamy tomatillo sauce are all very good. Service is excellent. At lunch today, we were each sent home with a complimentary "worry doll" and a wrapped churros to go. Legend has it that Guatemalan children tell one worry to each doll when they go to bed at night then put the dolls under their pillow and in the morning the dolls will have taken their worries away.[24]

24. https://www.zomato.com/review/yweRNl.

CHAPTER 9

FOURTH INGREDIENT: EXPRESSION

"The manner of giving is worth more than the gift."

—Pierre Corneille

THE "HOW" OF A PURPLE GOLDFISH

The fourth of the R.U.L.E.S. is "expression." Expression speaks to "how you give" as opposed to "what you give." A Purple Goldfish is a beacon. It's a sign that shows you care. That little extra touch demonstrates that the customer matters.

OH, STEWARD...THERE'S A DINOSAUR IN MY ROOM

One of the signature elements of staying in a stateroom on a Carnival Cruise are the towel animals. Every night, guests return to their room to find one of the 40 different types of animals. A cruise favorite, the folks at Carnival create about seven million towel animals per year. Suffice to say; that's a lot of folding!

Several years ago, Carnival released a book called, "Carnival Towel Creations." The 88 pages encompass a "how to" manual on towel animal making. Think it's easy? New stewards at Carnival spend at least 10 hours of formal training to master the art of the fold. One of the things that we like about the towel animals is how Carnival has leveraged them across their various touch points. They've been the focus of advertising, PR, direct mail, and online. In other words, these towel animals literally have "legs."

IT'S NOT ABOUT THE MONEY

Treating guests as though they're a member of your family is a widely accepted, yet rarely implemented, hospitality principle. That's where the Custom Hotel in Los Angeles, California, has flipped the script. According to one TripAdvisor review:

> Three stays at the Custom Hotel in LA, and we have nothing but GREAT things to say about the hotel, staff, cleanliness, service, food, and drinks from LA

Blues. It starts as soon as you get off the flight (ours was returning from Santiago, Chile) and the ground transportation is there in a manner of minutes, and Prince (just kidding, Trent) was very cordial and versatile! The hotel staff greeting us at the desk always treats us like family, and if I go on anymore, anyone reading this will think that I got compensated for my review.

Custom doesn't need to advertise itself as a "family feeling" establishment. If you have to wear it on your sleeve that much and tell others then you're doing what really matters; taking the action to convey it. Custom shows that the proof is in the pudding and lives by the adage, "What you do speaks so loudly that I cannot hear a word you say."

CURBSIDE: A LOST ART

Tenders Fresh Food in Cornelius, NC, is a fast casual restaurant that's famous for opting for the classic 1950's "hamburger joint" approach (though they're a chicken operation) complete with drive-up curbside service rather than a drive-thru. According to the operating director, Justin Trask:

> People, young and old, absolutely love our curbside pick-up service. All guests need to do is pull their car up into one of our three lanes, and one of our team members comes out to meet them in the rain, sun or snow. What the team is complimented the most on is their hustle though. Imagine someone literally running out to your car to greet you with a huge smile to take your order and then hustling back to the building to double-check your order and then run it back out to you. It's a lost art in our industry. Not only that, I

believe that people are tired of the "tip culture" where a tip jar is placed on virtually every counter for every service without them having to do much. When you see someone hustling, sweating, and grinding to serve you; a few bucks to reward them is gladly given.

JUST "BE THERE"

Stan's friend, Stephanie Hadden, his this to add about the Four Seasons Hotel, "When you check in, the front desk attendant will walk around to the front of the counter and hand you your key while using your name and anticipating your every need. This customer service costs them nothing extra but makes you feel like a million bucks."

Purple Goldfish Takeaway: You don't have to tap into money to go the extra mile. Being quick, responsive, and alert with your customer service can make all the difference.

CHAPTER 10

FIFTH INGREDIENT: STICKY

"Why wait to be memorable?"

—Tony Robbins

STICKY = WORD OF MOUTH

The fifth of the R.U.L.E.S. is the concept of being "sticky." You want an experience that "sticks" in the mind of consumers and promotes word of mouth. Ultimately, creating an experience and providing services that are both memorable and remarkable (thus worth talking about). Two questions to ask yourself about a proposed idea:

1. Is it water cooler material?

2. Will your customer tell three people or 3,000?

WHAT IS A KAMADO?

Brooks had the pleasure of starting a restaurant concept in Raleigh, NC, called Kamado Grille. You might find yourself asking what exactly a kamado style grill is, and you're certainly not alone. "Kamado" is a Japanese word that means "ceramic cooking oven" and the grills have been popularized by brands such as the Big Green Egg of Atlanta, GA. The Kamado Grille team noticed right away that guests referred to their Kamado Joe (a Big Green Egg competitor) grills as "eggs" and knew that they need to put a special emphasis on the word, "kamado."

To help familiarize guests with the brand and concept of kamado style cooking, the Kamado Grille team instituted some added features to help tell their story and the history of the grill:

1. Two sets of four 42 inch TVs that all work in unison to show live feeds from the five cameras placed around the kitchen. The TVs help show the grills in motion and the team hard at work.

2. Full tours from the management and ownership of the entire restaurant and the kitchen. The end of the tour often comes with a magnetic Kamado Grille pin.

3. Free cooking classes every Saturday at 10:00 AM where all attendees are provided complimentary soft drinks and can try an existing, or potential, menu item. They also live stream the cooking class for those unable to attend.

4. Kamado Grille will print off or email any of their recipes for a guest that shows interest.

5. Brooks and the executive chef, Eric Gephart, often welcomed fan questions via social media and answered all of them on YouTube.[25]

6. The team filmed a weekly video newsletter around the restaurant's happenings and started out every episode with a fan giveaway.

7. Kamado Grille often paired up with charities to create special menus and donated 100% of the proceeds back to the charitable organization.

Kamado Grille hones in on one word that explains their experience, "significant." With remarkable giving and a commitment to serving others with the heart of a servant, that's just the word that should be used to describe the new restaurant chain.

I NEED A STEAK...ON THE DOUBLE

Bestselling author and speaker, Peter Shankman, tweeted at the Morton's Steakhouse chain a tongue-in-cheek comment about

---

25. bit.ly/KamadoQuestions

needing a great steak dinner when his flight landed. According to Shankman:

> As I've tweeted and mentioned countless times before, I'm a bit of a steak lover. I go out of my way to try steakhouses all around the world when I can, and it's one of the reasons, no doubt, that my trainer at my gym is kept in business. But it's all good - give and take. Over the past few years, I've developed an affinity for Morton's Steakhouses, and if I'm doing business in a city which has one, I'll try to schedule a dinner there if I can. I'm a frequent diner, and Morton's knows it. Back to my flight. As we were about to take off, I jokingly tweeted the following:
>
> Hey, @Mortons, can you meet me at Newark airport with a porterhouse when I land in two hours? K? Thanks :-)
>
> Walking off the plane, I headed towards the area where the drivers wait, as my assistant Meagan had reserved me a car home. Looking for my driver, I saw my name, waved to him, and started walking to the door of EWR like I'd done hundreds of times before. "Um, Mr. Shankman," he said. I turned around. "There's a surprise for you here." I turned to see that the driver was standing next to someone else, who I just assumed was another driver he was talking to. Then I noticed the "someone else" was in a tuxedo. And he was carrying a Morton's bag.

Shankman immediately expressed his excitement and delight via social media and subsequently wrote a blog post that instantly went viral. When we talk about reaching the masses with a little token of appreciation, this is exactly what we're referring to. Morton's didn't ask that Shankman share the story. Shankman did so under his own volition because he was so excited about the unexpected gift and the story will continue to be told for years to come.

DROPPING THE STICKY BOMB

Phil Gerbyshak nominated AJ Bombers of Milwaukee, Wisconsin, as a true "sticky" experience. In Phil's words:

> One of my favorite Purple Goldfish is AJ Bombers in Milwaukee. Joe Sorge and his team consistently provide the Purple Goldfish by offering free peanuts...shot at you in metal WWII bombers. It's way fun to get those from the bartenders. Making AJ Bombers even more fun is the fact that Joe is on Twitter, recognizing customers and anyone who mentions the place, hosts Tweetups at Bombers, has guest bartenders where he donates shots folks can sell...with all proceeds going to the charity of the guest bartender's choice.
>
> Full disclosure: I've been a guest bartender and raised money for my charity. Last, but certainly not least, is that all guests can snag a Sharpie and put their Twitter handle anywhere they want at AJ Bombers. This way, when friends come in, they can look for your Twitter handle and leave you a tweet...in real life.

Do you believe in love at first sight? We do now. We're huge Five Guys fans because of the free peanuts. In fact, we put Five Guys in the Purple Goldfish Hall of Fame based on their peanuts and the handfuls of extra fries. AJ Bombers takes the peanut to the next level! Move over "El Muchachos Cinco," you've got some company.

Of the five main ingredients or R.U.L.E.S., Bombers scores huge on stickiness. As Phil mentioned, the bartenders send bombers attached to rails above the bar to deliver the peanuts.[26] The owner, Joe Sorge, emailed us and added an interesting wrinkle, "Not only do we offer free peanuts to our guests while they are at the restaurant, they always get bonus nuts with all 'to go' orders. Their reactions are priceless; they love it."

Here is a rundown of the top five from AJ Bombers:

- **P-nut Bomber** – A signature way to deliver peanuts to the respective booths in the restaurant.

- **Oversized Beach Chairs** – A couple larger than life beach chairs. You feel like a silly little kid while sitting in an enormous chair but, then again, isn't that the point?

- **Quad Cow** – Many extreme eaters take on the "quad cow" challenge at AJ Bombers. After you've swallowed the last bite of your four patty burger, you can sign your name on the sacred cow that adorns the wall.

- **Sharpies** – Grab a marker and leave your name or Twitter handle on the wall. You are now part of AJ Bombers.

- **Streamlined menu** – Your menu is a narrow piece of paper that details the various burgers and also allows you to customize your meal as you deem fit. Grab a pencil and start choosing but with their plethora of toppings, our advice is to choose wisely.

A REAL PURPLE COW

Phil Gerbyshak also shared another gem from Milwaukee, WI:

> I was just thinking about one of my favorite Milwaukee Purple Goldfish, Pizza Shuttle. From the original

---

26. https://www.youtube.com/watch?v=KB6Zrvf-Ifs

Andy Warhol "Purple Cow" in the dining area, to the fantastic hold messages, to the old Pizza Shuttle trading cards they let people collect of their drivers, to the fact you get free pizza on your birthday, to the in-store photo booth perfect for taking pictures; it's all fun. Couple that with the late-night delivery of pizza AND frozen custard AND chicken AND burgers, fun, unique people who work there and you get an amazing place to eat and an experience for everyone. A few other wonderfully inventive things they do: The world's largest pizza, available for dine-in only; An amazing program where they give back HUGE to the community they serve; Delivery to all the colleges, hotels, and universities in the area; Employing nearly 100 people in a town that can desperately use it.

We find that businesses that tend to get the concept of lagniappe usually have several Purple Goldfish included in their experience. These entities understand that to stand out you need to differentiate by giving those little unexpected extras and Pizza Shuttle is no exception. Here is a summary of Pizza Shuttle's top five Purple Goldfish:

1. **The Purple Cow** (hat tip to Seth) – How many pizza places have a framed Andy Warhol on display? The genius interplay of pop culture and an homage to the dairy state of Wisconsin.

2. **A Picture Booth** – Take your experience home with you with a branded strip of black and white photos. A great memento for a date with your squeeze or a night out with your friends. A picture may be worth a thousand pizzas.

3. **The Largest Pie in Wisconsin** – Be memorable by offering a $39.95 gut buster. According to an article by Jason McDowell, they also throw in the ice cream as an added lagniappe.

4. **Free WiFi** – This is becoming a no brainer as of late. But how many pizza places offer complimentary wireless access and actually want guests to hang around?

5. **Unique Hold Music** – Imagine actually wanting to be put on hold. Smart move when you have a robust delivery business. Create some fun messages so people can be entertained while they wait.

PROMOTING WORD OF MOUTH WITH SPARE CHANGE

Here's an example from Ben Popken at *The Consumerist*:

As a favor to guests, one hotel washes every coin it receives, just like it has been done since 1938. The practice at the St. Francis Hotel in San Francisco is said to have started when hotelier Dan London observed that some coins sullied a woman's white gloves. At the time, coins were used for everything from tips to payphones to taxicabs. Back then, washing the coins was a full-time job. Now it's only a few hours a week, but the practice continues, passed down from one generation to the next.

The coins are first passed from the general cashier to the coin washer who dumps them into a silver burnisher. Along with the coins, the burnisher is filled with water, buckshot to knock the dirt off, and a healthy pour of 20 Mule Team Borax soap. After three hours of swishing the coins around, the hotel staff uses a metal ice scoop to pour the loot into a perforated roast pan that sifts out the buckshot. The wet coins are then spread out on a table beneath heat lamps. This is where once-rusted copper pennies turn into shim-mering bronze coins. Quarters look like sparkling sil-ver bits.

Lagniappe Takeaway – Do guests of the St. Francis care that their coins are sparkly? Other than the germophobes... probably not. But this Purple Goldfish ranks extremely high on sticky. In essence, shiny coins are worth talking about!

BE A NINJA FOR A NIGHT

A lot of "tourist trap" restaurants that attract the masses because of their unique offering are ripped mercilessly on Yelp. Try taking a gander at the reviews of South of the Border in Dillon, SC, or Casa Bonita in Lakewood, CO. Perhaps it's because consumers have such high expectations after hearing so much about the "remarkable" ex-perience and their sights are set unrealistically high.

That's where Ninja New York turns high expectations on its head. Here's how the president of Ninja New York, Haruo Yazaki, ex-plains the different experience that they aim to create:

> I am very proud to introduce the "NINJA," a time-hon-ored Japanese culture, to all those in New York. Once you set foot in our restaurant, you will be pulled into a world beyond your imagination. It will be our pleasure if we should succeed in "impressing" our customers. Dishes that are pleasing to the eye and also tasty; qual-ity service, surprises, and an accurate recreation of the NINJA castle.

Yes, you read that correctly, Ninja New York is a restaurant that aims to recreate a day in the life of the Japanese ninja. Here's what our friend, Steve Magnolia, had to offer about his experience:

When you enter the restaurant, there are two paths you get to choose from: the regular path or the ninja path. We entered on the street level and then were taken on an elevator down into the ninja dining level. There were some actors/waiters hiding in the stairways that jumped out to scare us. It was pretty awesome!

Most of the tables are secluded, but we ended up getting a little cave. What kind of restaurant has personal caves? The whole restaurant is set up like a Japanese Ninja village, and many dishes are served with Ninja performances such as being cut with a sword, having the dish served on fire or food being served over dry ice. How cool! They even present the menus to you in a scroll. A magician [or ninja I guess?] came to our table and asked us if we would be interested in some card tricks and a magic show. At what other restaurant would you see this?

Also, I didn't know that having your back turned to the performers and your "table ninja" (i.e. your server) enables them to scare the crap out of you but I found that out the hard way. After about the third time I was "stabbed" I understood that I needed to have my guard up. It was hilarious and very entertaining, and I can't stop talking about it, so I guess their approach worked!

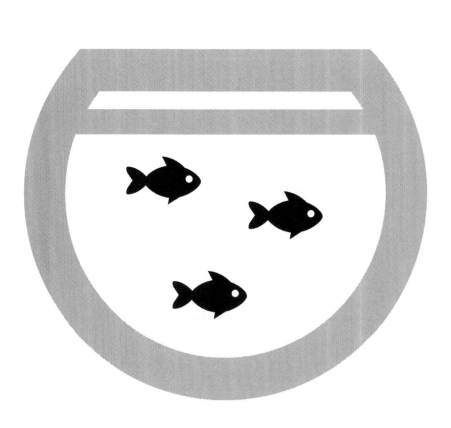

PART III

12 TYPES OF PURPLE GOLDFISH

CHAPTER 11

THE VALUE/ MAINTENANCE MATRIX

"There are no traffic jams along the extra mile."

—Roger Staubach

ARE YOU DOING THE LITTLE THINGS?

" Giving Little Unexpected Extras" (GLUE) show that you genuinely care about the people that you serve. There are a dozen
different types of Purple Goldfish that can be provided as a
lagniappe. Half are based on "value" and half are based on "maintenance" according to the value/maintenance matrix. Think of
value as the enhancement of the experience and maintenance as
the support of an ongoing relationship.

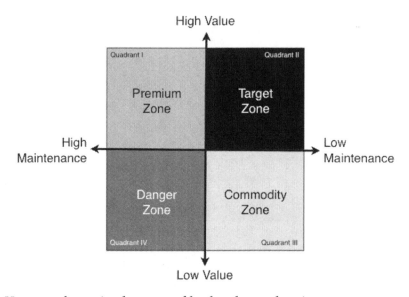

Here are the main elements of both value and maintenance:

Value (the "what" and "when" of customer experience)

- What are the benefits your service or product provides?

- Does your offering go above and beyond to exceed customer
  expectations?

- Are you giving that little unexpected extra to surprise and delight your customer?

Maintenance (the "who" and "how" of customer experience)

- What is the buying experience like for your customer?

- Do you make things turnkey or simple for your customer?

- Are you responsive to the problems your customer encounters?

12 CATEGORIES

#1. Throw-ins (value) – Little extras that are included with your product or service. They help you stand out in a sea of sameness:

> Example: Southwest Airlines is famous for its "Bags Fly Free" and no change fees.

#2. In the Bag / Out of the Box (value) - Little unexpected things that are added as a surprise to delight consumers.

> Example: Maggiano's encourages guests to order a pasta dish and Maggiano's will pack an additional one up for you to take home on the house.

#3. Sampling (value) - Give your customer an additional taste by offering a free something extra on the house.

> Example: At Izzy's, order an ice cream cone and get another scoop of ice cream on top for free.

#4. First & Last Impressions (value) - You have two chances to make an impression. When your customer comes through the door and right before they walk out, hang up or log off. These little extras make you memorable, and more importantly, talkable.

Example: When you check into the Hard Rock Hotel, they will let you rent a Fender guitar. Check in, plug-in, and rock out!

#5. Guarantees (value) - Give your customers that little extra pledge that you'll stand behind your product or service.

Example: The 100% Hampton Inn Guarantee offers guests their money back if they're unsatisfied for any reason.

#6. Pay it Forward (value) - Give a little extra back to the community.

Example: Rosa's Fresh Pizza offers its guests the ability to "buy a slice and give a slice" of pizza to a person in need

#7. Follow-up call (maintenance) - Make the little extra follow-up with your customer.

Example: Ritz-Carlton calls to thank their guests and sendsthem a handwritten thank you card after their stay.

#8. Added Service (maintenance) - The little extra that's an added unexpected service.

Example: At Fazoli's, the restaurant management serves guests out in the dining room rather than behind the counter.

#9. Convenience (maintenance) - The little extras you add to make things easier for your customers.

Example: Chick-fil-A encourages parents to place their order through the drive-thru so that their food and table are ready when parents come inside with their children.

#10. Waiting (maintenance) - All customers hate to wait. If it's inevitable, how can you do a little extra to make it more bearable?

Example: At Pacific Cafe, guests can enjoy a complimentary glass of wine while they wait for their table.

#11. Special Needs (maintenance) - Acknowledging that some customers have needs that require special attention.

Example: Rainforest Cafe caters to the needs of the customer by doing a little extra for those with food allergies.

#12. Handling Mistakes (maintenance) - Admitting that you're wrong and doing the little extra above and beyond to make it "more than right."

Example: Mellow Mushroom management is trained to apologize for any food mistake and remake the order with no questions asked.

CHAPTER 12

#1 - THROW-INS

"A fellow who does things that count,
doesn't usually stop to count them."

—Variation of a saying by Albert Einstein

VALUE YOU CAN ADD TODAY

The next six chapters in the book will cover the types of Purple Goldfish associated with "value." The first example of value comes to us in the form of "throw-ins." Throw-ins are the little unexpected extras that are included with your product or service. As we mentioned before, the lowest hanging fruit in marketing lagniappe is added value. Let's revisit a classic example.

SIGNATURE LAGNIAPPE: THE DOUBLETREE HOTEL

As we mentioned before, and you know if ever stayed at a Double-Tree by Hilton hotel, their differentiator: a warm, freshly baked chocolate chip cookie upon your arrival. The nostalgia probably already has you salivating, doesn't it? In fact, the DoubleTree cookie has become so famous that it even has its own website where they sell their cookies, doubletreecookie.com. According to the website:

> For more than 30 years, DoubleTree by Hilton hotels have been welcoming guests with a warm, chocolate chip cookie at check-in. A select group of bakeries around the world hold the secret recipe to ensure every guest gets the same, delicious cookie at every DoubleTree by Hilton hotel and resort.

In our estimation, DoubleTree's cookie stands alone for a multitude of reasons:

• A warm, chocolate chip cookie is typically nostalgic of childhood where you were rewarded for good behavior and marked a special occasion. This makes guests feel welcome, relaxed, and grateful for the gift that they have received.

- The warm sensation makes the gift feel homemade and as though the cookie was made especially for them.

- A chocolate chip cookie is simple, classic, and accommodates just about any taste.

- They were the first to give the gift. Everyone else is now just an imitator. Consumers think, "We get a cookie? Oh, that's what DoubleTree does." It's a kind gesture, but it actually might make guests think of another brand.

Are you smellin' what we're cookin' here? Let's look at some more examples of a throw-in.

DON'T WORRY. DESSERT IS ON US.

Jason's Deli is a fast casual delicatessen restaurant chain headquartered in Beaumont, Texas, that is known for their healthy sandwiches, soups, and salads. Jason's also features a full salad bar which can conveniently be paid for via credit card at a little kiosk and sits directly adjacent to a soft-serve machine. Why is there a soft serve machine in their dining room? That's because dessert is on the house. All Jason's Deli diners have the option of creating a chocolate, vanilla, or chocolate/vanilla swirl cone that they can eat at Jason's or take on the road with them.

According to Jason's website, "All the best meals end with dessert. That's why we offer free ice cream with every purchase. Stop by today and enjoy a cone (or a cup) on us." Theoretically, Jason's could be taken to the cleaners by not supervising the soft serve machine and allowing guests to take copious amounts of ice cream. However, it's this differentiator that causes many consumers to choose Jason's over any other sub shop. A little gift can truly make all of the difference.

A BOWLFUL OF QUARTERS

The etymology of Lagniappe stems from the Quechan *"yapay"* which means "to give more." Zane's Cycles of Branford, Connecticut, lives by this mantra and leverages customer service as the point of differentiation. A 30+ year veteran of the retail bicycle industry, Chris Zane has built Zane's into one of the largest bicycle stores in the nation by giving customers more than they expect. More importantly, Zane's stand behind the sale by providing more service than is reasonably expected (especially by competitors).

Zane's is willing to spend $100 to service a customer. To illustrate the point, Chris uses the metaphor of a bowl filled with 400 quarters. During presentations, Chris walks around with a bowl and encourages members of the audience to take quarters. Most only take a few quarters, but no one ever takes the whole bowl.

According to Chris, "The point is that when you as a customer are presented with more than what seems reasonable, like a bowl of 400 quarters, you will self-regulate. By providing more service than what folks consider reasonable, we can build trust and loyalty and remind them how hard we're working on their behalf."

Here are some of the compelling ways that Zane's offers little extras to maximize lifetime value:

1. **Free Trade-In Program for Kids** - Buy a bike for your child at Zane's. When they outgrow the bike, bring it back to trade-up. Zane's gives you credit for the price of the old bike towards a new one.

2. **Gift Certificates in Water Bottles** - Buy a gift certificate and Zane's will throw in a complimentary branded water bottle that holds the certificate. Simple but effective.

3. **The One Dollar Rule** - Zane's doesn't charge for any parts that cost them one dollar or less. Need a master link for your chain? It's on the house. In fact, they typically will throw in an extra master link as a lagniappe.

4. **Coffee Bar** - Zane's has an awesome espresso bar in the store encouraging customers to sit down, relax, and enjoy a cup of gourmet coffee.

5. **Set of Small Tools** - Zane's provides a complimentary toolkit when shipping bikes to recipients.

6. **Webcam** - Zane's has a camera in the repair shop which gives customers the ability to Skype with the repair team.

7. **Personal Notes** - Each person who buys a bike receives a handwritten thank you note.

8. **Test Rides** - Want to test a bike at Zane's? You're free to take it out for a ride. No credit card or driver's license required. Each year they lose a handful of bikes, but the small cost is insignificant compared to the trust gained when hassle has been avoided.

YOU ARE NOW FREE TO CHANGE YOUR TRAVEL PLANS

Southwest Airlines stands for "freedom" in air travel. Following up on the successful "Bags Fly Free" program, Southwest introduces the next chapter in eliminating fees. Southwest created a policy that states, "No charge for change fees at Southwest. Saving customers upwards of $150." At Southwest "fees" are a four letter word and a very bad one for that matter. Here is a rundown of how Southwest treats fees:

• No first or second checked bag fees

- No change fees

- No fuel surcharge fees

- No snack fees

- No aisle or window seat fees

- No curbside check-in fees

- No phone reservation fees

Lagniappe Takeaway: Fees don't fly at Southwest. Sometimes providing a lagniappe is not about what you give, but rather what you decide not to charge for.

CHANNEL YOUR INNER ROBIN HOOD

A bow and arrow aren't just tools for William Tell. At the Four Seasons Resort Lanai in Hawaii, you are invited to try your hand at archery or clay shooting for a chance to win a prestigious crystal pineapple. Here's a review from TripAdvisor, "My son and I enjoyed going to the shooting range and taking a lesson with the air rifle, followed by target practice and each of us winning a crystal pineapple for our accuracy during the shooting contest. The instructor, Reno, was very friendly and made the experience memorable for us."

A JELLY BEAN AND HUGE SCOOPS

Stan's friend, Jody Padar, provided a description of Wilson's ice cream store:

> At my favorite ice cream store in Door County, Wisconsin, they put a jelly bean at the bottom of the ice

cream cone, so it doesn't drip. They also give the biggest scoop ever. It's tradition. The girls who scoop the ice cream live upstairs. There is never a night in the summer where the line is short, and everyone happily stands on the porch waiting. They were featured on the Travel Channel and were sold recently for a few million dollars. Not bad for an ice cream store.

DISHING OUT THE CHOWDER

Myrtle Beach, SC, may be Mecca if you are a fan of playing golf. Take your pick of roughly 125 courses within a 25-mile radius. With so many choices, though, how do you stand out in the "sea of sameness" as a local golf course? Enter Caledonia Golf & Fish Club in Pawleys Island, South Carolina. Built in 1995, Caledonia has quickly earned a top billing.

In the words of our friend, Jeff Day, "Caledonia Golf & Fish Club offers a cup of chowder at the turn, which is cooked and served right in front of you on the tenth tee – it's a unique experience. Also, on Thursdays, the course hosts a collegial public fish fry on the grounds for players to relax, eat and mingle, sharing glowing reviews of their day."

A LITTLE TASTE AND SOME EXTRA SAUCE

Fast-casual chicken chain, PDQ, based out of Tampa Bay, FL, is known to attract some lines that run out the door. While their guests wait, PDQ often provides samples of their in-house baked cookies or homemade lemonade. The main difference maker is the eight different dipping sauces that PDQ makes in-house. According to the Lakeland, FL, operating director, Drew Zaras:

I know that our guests love that we don't charge them for extra dipping sauces. Our competition always seems to try and nickel and dime their customers for extras and we'll never do that. Fair value and an awesome experience every single time. For fast casual/quick serve, you just can't beat PDQ in this regard.

ANYONE FOR SALSA?

This Purple Goldfish was submitted by Stan's friend, Jordan Stark. It's simple, but it's still a great catch:

I recently grabbed lunch a Moe's Southwest Grill and was pleased to find that with any of the meals you order that you are given free tortilla chips and then can pick from four or five different types of salsa. This may not sound like much but over at Chipotle, the most comparable quick-food Mexican restaurant, that would cost you $2.50. Who doesn't love some free chips and salsa with their meal?

A LITTLE EXTRA ON THE "SLIDE"

This example slides in from a post by Colin Shaw of Beyond Philosophy:

Sometimes, the best ideas are the simplest ones. Inside Singapore's Changi Airport there is a four-story slide. What on earth is a slide doing in an airport? Simple – it's putting a bit of fun back into the customer experience. Spend 30 SGD within the airport, and in return, you get two slide tokens. This is a great way of rewarding customers who would most likely be shopping within the airport regardless and thus turning a boring time spent waiting around, into a surprising, rewarding and entertaining experience.

Isn't this a bit exclusive I hear you ask? What if you don't want to pay for that overpriced cup of coffee? Well, there's the smaller but free one-and-a-half story slide for the more frugal airport customers.

VIVA LAS FRENCH FRIES

Taken from a restaurant review in the *Las Vegas Review Journal*:[27]

If you're even slightly tuned in, you're no doubt aware that Michael Mina is widely regarded for his skills as a chef, most notably with fish and seafood. But you may not know that he rocks french fries and onion rings. No lie, french fries and onion rings, two of the standouts of our recent dinner at Stripsteak at Mandalay Bay. The skillful preparation of them proved why these two simple things — often deservedly scorned — have solid footholds in the culinary landscape.

The French fries were a lagniappe, served shortly after we ordered our wine. Fried in duck fat, they had an extreme crispness that sharpened the contrast to their fluffy interiors. They were served as a trio (a favorite Mina conceit) with one portion dusted with smoked paprika and served with barbecue sauce, one served with aioli, the other with homemade ketchup. Servers at Stripsteak point out that entrees are served a la carte, but with a lagniappe as generous as this, that point is easy to argue.

27. http://www.reviewjournal.com/entertainment/restaurants/stripsteaks-careful-preparation-shows-even-simple-things-perfectly

HAVE A CHOCOLATE OR THREE

The Ghirardelli Ice Cream & Chocolate Shop chain is notorious for giving out copious amounts of chocolate samples on the street (even if the consumers don't venture into the store). According to one TripAdvisor reviewer in Orlando, FL:

> My kids came here for ice cream a lot. Every time we visited they gave us free chocolates. We got to try a huge selection as we were at Disney for two weeks. Everything we tried was yummy.

According to another online Yelp review, "Everyone goes here for the free samples of chocolate. It is nice to be able to try different kinds. We always get a bag or two!!! Yum Yum!!" The last sentence encapsulates our main point. Satisfied guests and the principle of reciprocity through a throw-in are helping to boost Ghirardelli's top-line.

A SWEET HAND-SPUN EXTRA

Submitted via email by Matt Sheehan of *The Good Men Project*. In Matt's words:

> I was out to dinner in the Back Bay last week, and I had a head-on collision with a Purple Goldfish. Lolita, a hot new Mexican restaurant and tequila bar on Dartmouth and Boylston, gives free cotton candy with your bill at the end of the meal. They also give you a complimentary grapefruit and tequila flavored shaved ice palette cleanser when you first arrive at your table.

25% OFF FOR LIFE

The Ohio-based Melt Bar & Grilled restaurant chain offers a very special ongoing benefit for its guests: 25% off for life. Considering that food cost usually runs between 20-35%, how can Melt possibly afford to give guests 25% off of their bill? The catch is, the guest must get a "Melt" tattoo. According to Melt's website:

> Check out our tattoo gallery to see all the great designs so far and get some ideas for your Melt tattoo. Feel free to contact us for suggestions or approvals before getting the tattoo work done (remember, this is permanent!) We can also suggest great shops to get your custom work done. After the tattoo is complete, bring yourself and your new tattoo in for a few photos. We will you an official tattoo number and present you with your Melt Tattoo Family card which unlocks the benefits of being a member...25% off any purchase at Melt Bar and Grilled for life!

If you don't mind being a walking and talking billboard for Melt, that's a heck of a cool deal and certainly a valuable throw-in!

A FREE PIZZA...AND MAKE IT SNAPPY

It seems that anyone that has ever been to Brooklyn, NY, felt compelled to recommend the Alligator Lounge where the pizza is always on the house. Here is a snippet from the NY Magazine's Karen Hudes on the Lounge:

> Inside what was once the Galleria pizza place, this bar's turquoise walls, pink flamingos and Romanesque details don't quite gel, yet one crucial feature remains intact: the arched, wood-burning oven. Because of the owners' sensational idea of serving free personal piz-

zas every night until 3:30 a.m., this unremarkable joint has turned into a lovable hangout that's a great first or last stop while barhopping. Young and old Williamsburg folk congregate along the bar, in the maroon, open-angle vinyl booths, and around the green pool table. A booming jukebox and Big Buck Hunter Pro game in back provide entertainment. A selection of 10 draft beers compliments the delicious crisp-crust pies, which are on the house with every drink; toppings like pepperoni, caramelized onions and flavorful sweet sausage are available for an extra $2.

After perusing the comments section from the article, we came across a cool testament from a consumer standpoint:

I don't want the place to get so crowded that I can't get in. This is a fantastic place, with Widmer Hefeweizen on tap, and of course...free pizza. I didn't know about the pizza when I wandered in mid-week. When the bartender told me about it, I pictured pizza pockets... but it's wonderful wood oven thin crust pizza.

You pay two bucks for your first topping and one buck for after that. I had mine loaded, so it set me back five dollars. The same pizza in Manhattan would have set me back 15 bucks. Would I be back? I'm thinking of getting an apartment above the place!

YOUR CHOICE: COFFEE OR ICE CREAM?

Stew Leonard's is a grocery store and restaurant without peer. It personifies the concept of lagniappe. There are a handful of extras the store offers, but our favorite is the free ice cream or coffee with a purchase of $100 or more in groceries. It's that little extra or

"WOW" according to Stew that makes all the difference. Stan had the opportunity to hear Stew recount a great story about the power of word of mouth:

> About 40 years ago, Stew was asked by the local elementary school to come out and speak on Career Day. The principal asked him to talk about the dairy business. As Stew pulled into the parking lot he saw a fire truck parked in front of the school with kids all around it. When he walked through the front door of the school, he saw a room about the Air Force playing a movie with jet airplanes. It was filled with kids. Across the hall was a police officer and he was showing a packed classroom about various police equipment and weapons.
>
> Soon he walked down the hall and found his classroom with a sign on the door that read "THE MILK BUSINESS." Stew walked in the room to find only three kids sitting there, two of which were the sons of one of his managers. For the next 30 minutes, he talked about the dairy business and running a store. At the end of the talk, he thanked the kids, reaching into his pocket and handing them each a coupon for a free ice cream.
>
> The kids left and Stew waited in his classroom for the second of the two Career Day sessions. He waited and waited...no kids. After a while, the principal came rushing in, "Stew...I don't know what you told those kids, but we have to move your next session to the school auditorium."

A SCHOOL OF FLYING PURPLE GOLDFISH

JetBlue builds value into their flight offerings. They know the little things can make the biggest impact. They understand it takes more than the proverbial half can of soda. Let's look at each differentiator:

- A full can of soda and unlimited brand name snacks. What's with the cup of ice with just a little bit of soda in it by other airlines? You feel jipped, and you certainly wouldn't put up with that treatment on the ground.

- First bag free. Southwest has done an amazing job of promoting that "Bags Fly Free," but JetBlue is singing from the same prayer sheet. Saving customers up to $100 per round trip is an added value.

- 36 channels that allow you to watch...when you want to watch them. JetBlue gives you the two things that traditional air travel takes away: choice and control.

- The most legroom in coach. Since Stan is over six feet tall, he can tell you that this component is essential. There is nothing more annoying than the person in front of you reclining into your kneecaps!

- Direct flights. Avoiding layovers is key. It saves time, hassle and annoyance.

A B&B THAT STUDIES THE ART

The Seavey family takes hospitality seriously and over-delivering at their bed and breakfast, Her Castle, is priority number one. According to Bill Seavey:

> We run a home-based B&B, and we studied B&B's for several years before we became one--obviously

by staying in them. Homestays are much more personal and service-oriented. Our customers all get an hors d'oeuvre tray to their rooms upon arrival (along with wine, soda or fruit juice) which has a variety of cheeses, guacamole, candies, fruit, etc. People appreciate such luxuries after knocking the dust off from road trips.

My wife makes sure that there are signs or decorations in their rooms drawing attention to their birthdays or anniversaries. We try to accommodate people by making restaurant or wine tour reservations for them. We go over restaurant choices with them when they check in. We treat our guests with the adage, "a stranger is a friend we haven't met yet." Many of our customers do indeed become friends, and often, repeat customers.

The last line is what it's all about at the end of the day, isn't it? Serving others, making lifelong friends, and creating passionate repeat customers. Well done, Bill!

ONE MORE FLYING GOLDFISH FOR GOOD MEASURE

KLM gives Delft Blue Houses to customers who fly business class. What exactly is a "Delft Blue House" though? Here is a little additional background on the history of the houses courtesy of Theo Kiewiet:[28]

The KLM houses are presents to travelers aboard KLM flights in Business and Royal Class. They have been given over an extended period and thus have become collector items. There are currently over 90 dif-

---

28. http://www.theokiewiet.de/klm/history.htm

ferent types which are each individually numbered in order of release.

KLM started issuing these miniature bottles in 1952. Airlines were not allowed to give presents to their customers because of unfair competition. So, KLM had some Blue Delft houses made, and filled them with genever (gin). Then, of course, their competitors complained, "KLM ís giving presents to their customers." KLM said, "May we decide how we serve our drinks? Is there a law which tells me drinks have to be served in a glass?"

CHAPTER 13

#2 - UNEXPECTED EXTRAS

"Here is a simple but powerful rule: always give people more than what they expect to get."

—Nelson Boswel

IN THE BAG AND OUT OF THE BOX

The second type of Purple Goldfish involves those unexpected extras that surprise and delight the people that you serve. These are little things that are given without notice and genuinely "wow" the masses. The key is to make this signature unexpected extra an intricate part of your strategy thereby making it synonymous with your brand.

SIGNATURE LAGNIAPPE: FIVE GUYS

As we discussed earlier, Five Guys has instituted a number of Purple Goldfish into their business model. The lagniappe that appears to get the most attention are the extra fries that Five Guys dumps on top of your order and subsequently all over the inside of your brown paper bag with to-go orders. "Bag fries" (as they've come to be known) have garnered a ton of attention and differentiate Five Guys from every other fast food burger joint in town. Steve Strauss, from theselfemployed.com, had an interesting take and analysis of the Five Guys "bag fries" and recently said:

> Here's what they do: When you order some fries from the counter, the server dutifully takes their little paper fry bucket, fills it up, and then puts it in a paper bag. Then they take an even bigger scoop of fries and dump it into the bag, on top of the regular order. I always think, and my kids always say, "I can't believe how many extra fries we get!"
>
> And then it finally dawned on me; we don't really get any extra fries at all, do we?
>
> The genius of this little show is that for all intents and purposes, it looks and feels like we get extra fries and that the guys and gals at Five Guys are being cool and

generous. However, upon a little post-carb reflection, the truth is that they planned on giving that amount of fries out regardless, and budget for that.

Steve presents an interesting point, and he's right, Five Guys does budget for the fries that are being "given away." If you recall from our analysis of Five Guys earlier, owner Jerry Murrell does not believe in advertising by and large. Instead, Murrell prefers to give a little extra to get customers to talk about them. However, just because you're providing a lagniappe does not mean that it has to be a cost that is not accounted for. Ultimately, Five Guys has taken a gift and turns into a fiscally responsible lagniappe that simultaneously perpetuates word of mouth advertising.

NOT YOUR AVERAGE SLEEP MENU

Pillow menus have become very common in hotels, and the premise is simple, let guests know what types of pillows you offer to ensure their comfort. There's one hotel, Conrad, in Chicago, that thinks so big that they even created a website that summarizes their offering.

Conrad offers a full, complimentary pillow menu to accommodate their guests at ConradChicagoSleepMenu.com.[29] Conrad also offers a complimentary "double wake-up call" to ensure that you don't miss your alarm as well as a "room refresh" where they will draw the curtains, turn the bedding back, and replenish water bottles in the room. Not only is their menu sizably larger than most competitors but they also offer virtually any other amenity that you can imagine including "sleep chocolate," H20 hydrating treatments, sleep sound machines, herbal sleep elixirs, and much more.

---

29. http://conradchicagosleepmenu.com/

ONE FOR THE ROAD

Maggiano's Little Italy certainly does not feel like a major restaurant chain as they offer family-sized portions that can be freely shared amongst a table. It seems like a meal at home without the corporate cost-cutting. The differentiator that Maggiano's has become known for though is their take-home entree portions that they pack up for departing guests. According to reader, David Zendel:

> I recently had a work meeting and chose Maggiano's and was pleasantly surprised to find that their meals were served family style. It's basically an all-out buffet without the hassles of one with way higher food quality. Conversations, both professional and personal, continued while we passed the platters and bowls of food to one another. It was like being home for Thanksgiving dinner, but we didn't have to cook!

> I also thought that the family style servings provides an opportunity to try new menu items that you might not have already chosen. In essence, the conundrum that you often face is whether you play it safe or try something new and feeling ripped off because you didn't care for the meal. No one wants to feel like they're high maintenance in asking for something new.

> The biggest thing that I noticed was the staff encouraging us to order the special ahead of time so that they could bring a few extra entrees and packing them all up for everyone in our party to take home. I have never heard of a restaurant doing that before, and the surprise delighted everyone!

IT REALLY IS THE LITTLE THINGS

This story comes to us from Ted Coinè of switchandshift.com. Ted remembers the story about a talented waitress who went above and beyond to provide the unexpected:

> When we were new to Naples, Florida, and our daughters were only two and four, my wife Jane and I found a great Irish pub on Fifth Avenue (the Rodeo Drive of this posh town). With little kids, we had no interest in $80 steaks and fine dining, so McCabe's was perfect for us.
>
> Still, you don't expect five-star customer service in a pub, so we certainly weren't looking for it that day! That's why what our waitress, Jenny, did was so remarkable. Our youngest daughter, Maryn, was eating finger food with plenty of ketchup, and her hands were covered in yuck, as you'd expect.
>
> As we spoke with Jenny about our meal, she unconsciously pulled out a hand towel and wiped Maryn's hands clean, not breaking eye contact with us the entire time. About halfway into this, I suddenly noticed what she was doing and, as you'd expect, I thanked her profusely - no waiter or waitress had ever done anything like this in our four years as parents thus far, I can tell you! It turns out that Jenny wasn't a mother, but she had grown up with younger siblings. She truly hadn't even realized what she was doing until I brought it to her attention; once I did, she kept going while we spoke, demurely refusing to let us make a fuss over her.

Jenny said, "Oh, of course, it's nothing," but it was something very special indeed! You can't train people to give service extras like this; as Bruce Nordstrom remarked when asked who developed his store's famously-excellent sales clerks, it wasn't the employer, it was "their parents." The lesson, as Phil McCabe confirmed when I spoke to him about Jenny, is you must hire people like Jenny, people who sincerely care.

This is what I like to call the ninja power of unexpected service excellence: when you're ready for three-star service (as you would at a pub) and you receive five-star service instead, man, that differential will turn you into a brand advocate for life! Because of Jenny's exceptional care, we've recommended countless friends and acquaintances to go there over the years.

CHAMPAGNE, RESERVATIONS, AND MORE

The Halkin by COMO hotel in London, England, is known for delighting its guests in unconventional ways. According to one TripAdvisor reviewer, "We received a bottle of champagne for my wife's birthday, I assume it was for that reason as it was not detailed why. It was a bottle of Louis Roederer champagne and not a cheap substitute as you get in a lot of hotels which shows the class of the hotel." According to another TripAdvisor reviewer:

> We booked the hotel for our wedding anniversary. On making the booking the Concierge Team just couldn't do enough for us. Restaurants were recommended and booked every request was followed up instantly. On arrival everything was slick and the welcome...the glass of champagne was a lovely touch.

Typically a concierge team will make recommendations but to go above and beyond to make the reservations for guests is quite an unexpected bonus. Oh yes - and more free champagne! The Halkin is doing it right.

WHAT'S A JBPO?

JetBlue is famous for surprising its guests, but perhaps no example is as prolific as the "JetBlue People Officer" (JBPO). As Glen Stansberry of Gentlemint explained:

> If you fly JetBlue, you might just run into the mystical People Officer. One such passenger reports of the People Officer standing up mid-flight and announced that he had free tickets to give away to anywhere that the airline company flew. The man played trivia games and handed out tickets to anyone who knew the answers. In all, around a dozen free tickets were handed out during the mid-flight games. The JetBlue employee then went on to ask if anyone had any suggestions or concerns with JetBlue and answered questions about proposed upcoming promotions.

Lagniappe Takeaway: Surprising your customer with kind and relevant gifts is always a terrific business strategy. However, when you go out of your way to entertain them and show that you actually value their feedback; that's when a brand goes from great to iconic.

HAVE ONE ON US

Piada Italian Street Food is a fast-casual restaurant chain that is gaining a lot of traction. When stories like this one out of Worthington, OH, are as rampant as they are, this comes as no surprise. According to one guest from TripAdvisor, "My husband, son and I had a delicious dinner tonight BUT the gift was that it was an unexpected free dinner from the chef to us. I asked chef why and he said he likes to pick three people a day to give a free meal too - what an unexpected blessing his gift was to us."

JAY CUTLER DELIGHTS A LUCKY FAN

Serial entrepreneur, Gary Vaynerchuk, is known as being an audacious giver. What Vaynerchuk does with leveraging social media data to touch the hearts and minds of his customers is even more generous. When Vaynerchuk ran his family's $50 million wine business, he elaborated on a specific unexpected extra according to an article on rayhigdon.com:

> Gary had a guy buy $4,000 of wine from him and [found out that the customer] lived in Chicago. He decided to check this guy out and from examining the customer's Twitter account found out he was a Bears fan. As a total surprise, they sent this customer an autographed Jay Cutler jersey. Later the customer replied that he was blown away and had spent over a million dollars at his local wine supplier over the past 10 years but that they didn't even know his name let alone buy him any gifts. He told Gary that he would always buy all of his wine from him, and he has. Here's the even cooler part...four orders came in from other people that this customer had mentioned the jersey story to that totaled over $70,000!

Though Jay Cutler's jersey value has fallen a bit, imagine spending $200 and getting a $70,000 immediate return as a result. Not a bad deal for just appeasing a Bears fan.

[Note: Gary alluded that there might be some other 'branded acts of kindness' coming down the proverbial New Jersey Turnpike. Gary talked about the next major snow storm and the possibility of shoveling the driveways of his best customers. Imagine yourself as a customer and Gary shows up at your doorstep, shovel in hand. That's a Purple Goldfish we'd like to see.]

HAVE A CLOCK ON US

Gaylord Opryland Hotel in Nashville, TN, is a hotel known for its proximity to the sights and sounds of the city and surprising their guests. This comes to us from a post on Brand24:

> Christina McMenemy, who stayed at the resort three years in a row, was entranced with very specific spa-style music that the clock radio at the resort played. She desperately wanted to get a similar machine at her place, as every time she got back home from Gaylord Opryland hotel, she missed that light and relaxing music. During her most recent trip to Opryland, she asked the hotel on Twitter where could she get the amazing alarm clock, but it turned out that the machine is made just for the resort.

> Though a little bit disappointed, Christina appreciated Opryland's effort and gave up on hunting the dream clock. But to her surprise, when she got back to her room, she found two clock radios next to each other, along with a note saying, "We hope you enjoy these spa sounds at home."

SURPRISING THE BIRTHDAY BOY

Children can be tough to travel with, especially in nicer hotels. There aren't many "activities" for kids to enjoy, but that's where the Omni Hotel surprised and delighted Susan George. In Susan's words:

> I would like to recommend the Omni Hotel in Charlotte! We had to go for a cheerleading Competition there and it was my son's birthday so obviously, he did not want to go. I asked what activities they had for kids, and they inquired what the backstory was. I told them about my son's situation, and they inquired how old he was, any allergies, what he liked, and so forth.
>
> I didn't think much of the conversation but discovered that upon arrival that we had been comped a Jr. Suite room and it was decorated with balloons, streamers, a banner, a personalized cake, ice cream, and soda. They went over and beyond. It was our first stay at The Omni and I won't stay anywhere else in Charlotte or Atlanta. They made a crappy weekend much better for our son.

CHAPTER 14

#3 - SAMPLING

"One of the best ways to motivate consumers to try new products is through sampling. Once a consumer tries a new product through sampling, it's likely they will add it to their shopping list."

—Julie Hall

THE LOWEST HANGING FRUIT IN MARKETING

There may not be a more cost effective way for brands to drive purchase intent and conversion than sampling. The proof is in the numbers as highlighted in this article in *Brandweek*.[30] Here are the top two takeaways from the Arbitron survey:

1. 24% of consumers bought the product they sampled instead of the item they initially set out to purchase.

2. 35% of customers who tried a sample bought the product during the same shopping trip.

But why does sampling just have to be about the prospect? Why can't you leverage current customers with an additional little extra to increase satisfaction, drive retention, and promote word of mouth? That's exactly what we're going to to propose in this chapter.

SIGNATURE LAGNIAPPE: IZZY'S

Izzy's Ice Cream is an iconic ice cream store in St. Paul. The owner, Jeff Sommers, was told to do two things when he opened his shop:

1. Smile, and;

2. Give away samples.

Jeff disliked the idea of just giving away free samples, so he created his own wrinkle. Customers are allowed to add an "IZZY" scoop with each scoop purchased. It's a small scoop of any flavor that goes right on top of the scoop that they bought. This tactic is great for customers who can now take a "worry free" chance to try a new

---

30. http://old.radiocentrum.be/sites/default/files/product_sampling_study.pdf

flavor. It's a little extra that goes a long way. Don't take our word for it; Izzy's was recently voted the best ice cream shop in America by *Reader's Digest.*

WANT A SAMPLE? GIVE ME DATA!

Brooks helped start a restaurant concept called Kamado Grille in Raleigh, NC, and can testify to the benefits for strategically sampling such as through tasting events to help decide the seasonal menu. As Brooks explains:

> When we wanted to decide what menu items to put on each season, we invited strategic groups in to try and rate the new dishes and drinks. We had four focus groups which are as follows:
>
> 1. **Grill owners** - These were the people who had purchased a $1,000-$1,600 grill from us (there's a retail shop as well). Having the ability to try the newest menu items and drinks before everyone else free of charge was one of the selling points for the grill.
>
> 2. **Bloggers** - These were the local power users across Instagram, Facebook, Snapchat, Pinterest, and Twitter that I had identified. I never wanted the invitation to feel contrived (as though we only invited them to get a review) but virtually all of them whipped out their phones to take pictures and wrote about us regardless. It was not required but this was a great side benefit.
>
> 3. **Social media contest winners** - We shot a weekly video newsletter and often asked people to comment or share the posts to try and win an in-

vitation to the tasting. Hundreds of comments and shares later, let's just say that we got the exposure that we wanted.

4. **Friends and family** - These are the people that we knew would be the most candid and not hold back. Additionally, when you're starting a restaurant chain, you tend not to have a life, so it was nice to see them every now and again.

Once we had the different groups sample the food and provide their feedback, we placed all of the ratings into a Google spreadsheet and ran simple algorithms based on the data. It was a highly effective program, and we got the exact type of objective feedback that we needed to make future business decisions.

Yes, Kamado Grille gave away hundreds of dollars worth of food but also think about the goodwill, valuable data, and brand equity that was accrued. With this type of system in place, this allowed Kamado Grille to make objective decisions with their menu development and they built context with their key audiences for the long haul.

A BEIGNET WHILE YOU WAIT

The Wandering Moose food truck based in Raleigh, NC, has many added bonuses. One of the most prolific are the complimentary miniature beignets that the Moose provides to its customers waiting in line. Often these samples are provided to new customers or the "regulars" to greet them and give them a little something to snack on before they get down to business with their full meal. According to owner, Anthony Reid:

We thought it would be a cool way to get people to talk more about the food and perhaps start their appetites a bit. When this transitioned into a perk for the regulars, it seemed to catch on and be a differentiator that no other truck was offering. Also, we don't sell it, but we offer our bacon scraps to patron's canine friends. Even though the dogs can't buy anything (we haven't figured that part out yet), everyone seems to enjoy it.

FIND ONE YOU LIKE

This comes to us from our friend, Bryan Harris, who said:

Most of the craft beer shops and gastropubs that are popping up left and right have little bars for tasting. What's cool is that they'll typically have at least 5-10 unique beers on tap, and they'll let you try all of them. As a restaurateur, I've found that people are very particular about their beer and don't want to spend five bucks on something that they don't care for.

The shop that I frequent is called The Hop Yard in Raleigh, NC, and I think they're one of the best in the biz. They're constantly getting new draft beers in, and the bartenders and ownership are eager to give you samples of the newest beers and tell you all about them. It's an added "nicety" that I appreciate and always results in me spending an additional 10-20 dollars on a six pack when I'm going out the door.

A TOUR AND A BIT MORE

This was offered to us by Bruce Brizendine about Flying Dog Brewery in Frederick, MD. In Bruce's words:

Brewery tours are just the best. Not only do you learn new facts about the company and its history but you get to try a lot of beer (which is equally as great). You might not be interested in a particular style, but when you have a tour guide explaining the in's and out's of the product, it just makes it taste better.

One of the better tours in the area is at Flying Dog in Frederick. Not only are their products top notch but their guides are extremely knowledgeable, and you can tell that they're passionate about what they're doing. Ultimately, you get to try all of their products (that you probably wouldn't have tried otherwise at $10 per six pack), and you get a decent buzz on. At the end, you're led back to their tasting room and gift shop. I always end up spending more at the bar and buying something to commemorate the experience. It never fails.

Also, if you want a good laugh, look up Flying Dog's "old" slogan that they're not allowed to print on the bottles anymore. I say "old" because it's still the unofficial mantra that you shout during the entire tour. I'll give you a hint: "Good Beer, No [Dog Doo]."

SMELL, SEE, TOUCH, AND TASTE IT

In the words of our friend, Nicolas Nelson:

The Great Harvest Bakery is a relatively small franchise chain of wonderful American-style bakeries that is growing slowly on purpose–they want to make extra sure that every new Great Harvest Bakery is top notch and fully reflects the ethos of the original one.

Lagniappe is what Great Harvest Bakery is all about–
it comes across in a dozen ways. But the first one, any
visitor, will notice immediately is the free bread tasting every time you come in the door. Yep, everyone
who even stops by gets a free slice of their choice of
the day's fresh-baked bread. A generous free slice.

Whether or not you buy something. Whether or not
you even stay in the bakery after you take their bread.
Whether or not you say thank you. Free bread, every
visit! Of course, there's a catch: the bread is unbeliev-
ably good. That free slice of bread will convince you to
buy a whole loaf. We do, almost every week.

As a general rule, "People don't know what they like...they like what
they know." You need to figure ways to get people to try new products. Make it easy and risk-free. Great Harvest gets to pick the bread
of the day and let customers experience something new.

TRY IT AND YOU'LL BUY IT

Credit card processor, Upserve, cited a study out of Cornell University to validate the effectiveness of sampling amongst beer and wine
manufacturers. According to upserve.com:

In the wine industry, offering free samples is a different
process. Typically a winery will offer "tastings" where
interested guests can get a taste of the offerings. But
does this strategy entice tasters to buy? According to
a study conducted by Miguel Gomez, an assistant professor at Cornell University, tastings can turn a "satisfied customer" into a "highly satisfied customer." The
difference here, according to the study, "she (or he) is
likely to spend an additional $10 buying an extra bottle

of wine (with a probability of 93 percent), and to re-purchase wine in the future (92 percent probability)."

This study took a look at 12 wineries in the Finger Lakes region of New York. All wineries may not experience the same results, but the study concluded that tastings create brand loyalty and entice guests to return for more. A few key components of improving customer satisfaction during tastings from the study:

- Provide great service

- Create a pleasant atmosphere

- Make the tasting memorable

- Allow for properly executed retailing

- Have a protocol for tastings that are established and shared with guests before the tasting itself

CHAPTER 15

#4 - FIRST & LAST IMPRESSIONS

"We don't know where our first impressions come from or precisely what they mean, so we don't always appreciate their fragility."

—Malcolm Gladwell

THE POWER OF PRIMACY AND RECENCY

One of the foundations of the lagniappe is the idea of leveraging primacy and recency.[31] As an example, you've probably heard the fact that people tend to remember the first thing and the last thing they see. A ton of attention is paid to the importance of a first impression (primacy), but little is made of the last moment (recency).

The concept of doing a little unexpected extra at the time of purchase is a recency strategy. This is partly explained by Nobel Prize Winner, Danial Kahneman, as the "Peak-End Rule." Kahneman believes that we judge our past experiences almost entirely on how they were at their peak (whether pleasant or unpleasant) and how they ended.

According to *Forbes* columnist Dean Crutchfield, "Designing for the peak-end rule is another way of not focusing on what is less important, but about focusing on what brings the most value to the customer experience. In other words, make sure that your peak and end is memorable, branded, and differentiated."

You never get a second chance to make a first or last impression. In essence, you need to give the customer something to talk, tweet, blog, Yelp or post on Facebook about right before they leave, hang up or log out. If they have left and you have not accomplished this, then you're already losing.

SIGNATURE LAGNIAPPE: REAL-LIFE RECIPROCITY

Stan told Brooks about the Friedman and Rahman study that we mentioned earlier which measured the difference in consumer

---

31. http://psycnet.apa.org/journals/abn/59/1/1

spend when provided a greeting and gift. In Brooks' words, here's what he found out when he tested this theory:

When Stan told me about the scientific study years ago, I knew that I needed to apply it in the trenches at my operation. The greeting made perfect sense to me, and it was something that, coincidentally, we were getting ripped on in the feedback site that I had built. The first step was ensuring that every single guest was greeted with the "10 & 5 rule." The 10 & 5 rule is a hospitality principle where eye contact is made at ten feet along with a smile and a wave, and at five feet, the guests are engaged with a greeting and an open palm to shake their hand.[32]

The greeter also swung the door open for guests and guided their eyes with an eye level open palm rather than pointing (which is a Disney principle).[33] At this point, guests were greeted in line with a vanilla milkshake sample and could ask our FOH staff member any questions that they had about our menu, restaurant concept, and so forth. There were two interesting caveats that we added to the equation later on:

1. Training at the counter to ensure that the team consultatively sold the milkshake (i.e., "We hope you enjoyed our sample, would you like to try our signature milkshake?") into their order entry and accompanied it with the "Sullivan Nod." The Sullivan Nod is a hospitality sales technique coined by consultant Jim Sullivan, CEO of Sullivision. com, whereby the hospitality team member affirmatively nods their head up and down in a subtle manner while offering specific menu choices.

32. http://yourbrandvoice.com/10-5-rule-of-hospitality/

33. http://www.overentertainment.com/secret-facts-about-disneys-rules-for-their-employees

2. Our dining room attendants were trained to incorporate a "table visit sale" where they asked guests that had not purchased a milkshake whether they'd like to get "a shake for the road." We figured that putting the burden on the FOH employee to complete the transaction and run the milkshake would entice additional spending.

The net result is that the combination of the greeting, milkshake sample, consultative sale, and table visit approach resulted in 42.2% higher milkshake sales on the day. Imagine when your average spend per guest jumps from $7.56 to averaging over $10 because of the $3.50-$5.00 milkshake spend. Of course you need to account for the additional labor and food cost spend but, overall, this is a winning philosophy that can be applied to a multitude of products and business verticals.

CHECK IN AND ROCK OUT

The Hard Rock Hotel in Chicago, Illinois, has gone out of its way to make its guests feel welcome. Their signature greeting lies within their "Sound of Your Stay" program where the hotel will allow guests to rent a turntable or Fender guitar. There might be a $500 deposit, but that does not deter guests who are elated with the unique offering. According to one reviewer on TripAdvisor, "You can rent a Fender or mixing table for free which is cool but on top of it all, expect friendly smiles and quick service."

NOT YOUR ORDINARY WELCOMING

Josiah Mackenzie of Review Pro wrote an outstanding piece about the greeting and overall service model at the Andaz Hotel by Hilton. According to Mackenzie, "Hyatt's Andaz brand replaces the traditional front desk reception concept by having hosts circulate the lobby to meet guests as they walk in." Joe Brancatelli, a business travel columnist, observed:

> You're invited to sit down and are offered a complimentary glass of wine or a cup of coffee. (Andaz properties have a barista on duty 24/7 in a lobby café.) The host then completes the check-in on a tablet computer. When you're finished sipping and signing, the host escorts you to your room.

> "Andaz is about giving great service in a relaxed way," says Toni Hinterstoisser, general manager of the Andaz on Wall Street. "A host's job is very different as they are supposed to be like the conductor of a symphony. We want them to anticipate your needs when you check in, make you relaxed, and be the person that you call throughout your stay when you need help."

When thinking about intentional customer experience design, it's clear that Andaz has started with the guest at the forefront of their mind. Most companies will never take the time to think about the impact of their welcoming and how it makes their guests think, feel, and react. Andaz is an exception to the rule.

HOW TO GET TO #6 ON THE CONDE NAST READERS CHOICE "BEST" LIST

Answer: lots of amazing class and service that is first class. Mark Brooks wrote an excellent post about the Hotel Murano on LostRemote.com. Here is an excerpt:

> A friend of mine, Brian Forth, recently made a reservation at the Hotel Murano in Tacoma, Washington. After making the reservation, Brian tweeted about how he was looking forward to having a stay-cation

with his wife in honor of his birthday. When the couple entered the hotel, they were greeted by name and given an automatic upgrade at no charge. When they entered the room, they found a welcome package including gourmet cupcakes. Naturally, Brian tweeted some more about all the nice surprises.

Upon check-in, he inquired about whether the hotel shuttle would ferry he and his wife to a local steakhouse for dinner. Later, he posted the same question on Twitter. About three minutes afterward, the phone rang in his room, and the concierge informed him that the shuttle would be available whenever it was needed.

So Brian tweeted again. And the culmination of those tweets, from [Brian] a respected local business owner, had arguably more marketing power than any local advertisement the hotel could have purchased with the money they spent making Brian and his wife happy. Think about it: the cupcakes cost $5, the rest of it was just awareness and hustle.

This is a prime example of giving the people you serve something to talk about. Mark referenced how Hotel Murano was voted #6 on the Condé Nast Traveler's Reader's Choice list. Mark went on further to state that this distinction has puzzled many of the locals, especially those in Seattle, WA. This all begs the question, though, how do they do it?

The proof is in the pudding...or maybe in the cupcakes. The companies who understand lagniappe tend to get the little things right. Whether it's greeting a first time customer by name [we assume that Murano found Brian's picture via social media] to a complimentary room upgrade or a shuttle ride; the Hotel Murano gets it. By the way, in case a guest may feel that they're missing out on miles or points, just whip out another hotel loyalty card and the Hotel Murano will hook you up with some immediate swag.

SAY MY NAME, SAY MY NAME

In Dale Carnegie's classic book, "How to Win Friends and Influence People," Carnegie claims that a person's name is the sweetest and important sound in any language to them. Perhaps that's why Marriott stresses the importance of using the names of their guests as they arrive. According to our friend, Kristen Baughman, "The JW Marriott addresses their customers by name when they get to the counter. Apparently the valet crew asks for the name as guests arrive while they are helping them with their luggage and then radio the name with a brief description of the guest to the front desk. Virgin Airlines does this as well with their passengers."

Our colleague, Ted Rubin, echoed this strategy and sentiment with an example from Ritz-Carlton. According to Ted, "Ritz-Carlton rocks...they always give personalized service, just try to open your own door there, and see how many people on the staff call you by name."

SHHH...IT'S A SEACRET

Anyone that has ever been to Ocean City, MD, has most likely been to Seacrets: Jamaica USA. It's the 15th highest grossing bar/nightclub in America, and it's just incredible. There's sand, palm trees, floating rafts/lounge areas, an outdoor music stage, a bouncing dance floor in the club, and a bar around every corner. It certainly looks like a place you would find in the Caribbean rather than the Eastern Shore of Maryland.

Seacret's gets a poor reputation because it's a "must see" and it can be hard to live up to those expectations. Combine this factor with strong, frozen drinks, and people's propensity to stay in the sun all day. You can probably put two and two together to figure out that some debauchery may transpire. However, there's something about Seacret's that will really "wow" you if you pay attention. It's their people.

Obviously, the place makes an incredible first impression but when you're greeted by college kids from all over the country and a lot of different Europeans; it's a pretty cool thing. Their staff is incredibly inviting, and I've found out that they're from Minnesota, Florida or New York and yet others that hail from Ireland, Bulgaria, and Russia. They're all vested in telling you the stories about how they ended up there, how the palm trees are flown in, and the other "must see" places in town. It never fails to leave a lasting impact with guests.

SURPRISE...YOUR BILL IS HALF OFF

There is a chain of sushi restaurants in the Triangle of North Carolina called Neo Asia that offers two for one sushi at all times. They also do two for one special on certain items from the bar. Imagine getting a flight of sake wine, a large Sapporo beer, and two rolls of sushi for only $14.95. The first time you go, you think it's a mistake, but it ends up being a pleasant surprise.

"Half off" every day is a distinctive pricing model. Not only can it be great for business (if you can figure out how to make the margins work) but it makes your fans look like they're "in the know" and part of a secret society. You only see the discount when your bill is presented. Talk about delight for a first timer!

FROM START TO FINISH: GREATNESS

Courtesy of Neal Levene over at Simple Complexity:

The Airport Fast Park at the Baltimore Washington International Airport is a little different than other "park-n-ride" airport shuttles. When you enter their lot, an attendant greets you and shows you the best row to park your car, so you don't have to search for an open space. The shuttle meets you at your parked car so there's no waiting at a shelter. Then the bus driver helps you with your luggage, and if it's raining meets you with an umbrella.

While on the bus, the friendly driver actually talks to you, and on your way back the shuttle takes you directly to your car, with a complimentary bottle of water.

SPICY MAC, A TINFOIL SWAN AND OYSTER SHOOTERS

Tucked under the Morrison Bridge in Portland, OR, is a restaurant called Le Bistro Montage (LBM) that boasts a handful of Purple Goldfish. Here are three of Stan's favorites from LBM:

1. A signature dish called "Spam and Mac." Imagine that, macaroni and cheese paired with your favorite mystery canned meat. For a little "lagniappe" with the flavor (which you won't see on the menu), you can order it "spicy."

2. Oyster and Mussel Shooters – Slimy fellas served in a shot glass with some cocktail sauce and horseradish. Once ordered the waiter or waitress will immediately scream to the kitchen, "OYSTER SHOOOOOTER."

3. Your leftovers get wrapped up in tin foil. Move over, balloon animal guy, the staff at the Bistro will "WOW" you with their animals.

CHAPTER 16

#5 - GUARANTEES

*"Truth is that you don't know what is going to happen tomorrow.
Life is a crazy ride, and nothing is guaranteed."*

—Eminem

STANDING BEHIND YOUR PRODUCT OR SERVICE

The fifth type of Purple Goldfish involves "Guarantees." The little extra commitment that you will stand behind your product or service. This can come in the form of guaranteeing your products, services, satisfaction, and so forth.

SIGNATURE LAGNIAPPE: HAMPTON INN

Hampton Inn, of the Hilton portfolio, makes a very bold statement about their accommodations. From the Hampton Inn website:

> Friendly service, clean rooms, and comfortable sur-
> roundings, every single time. If you're not satisfied,
> we don't expect you to pay. That's our commitment
> and your guarantee. That's 100% Hampton. Our 100%
> Hampton Guarantee® is boldly etched on our front
> desk so that it is constantly visible to our employees
> and our guests. Our guarantee epitomizes the pride we
> take in our brand, our hotels, and our service to you,
> our guest. We'll do whatever it takes to make our guests
> feel welcome, relaxed, and completely comfortable.[34]

It seems simple but clearly articulating such an ironclad guarantee helps put people's minds at ease. Whether consumers realize it or not, having an "out" or other option available makes them more likely to commit to an action. If you're that confident in your offering then what do you have to lose (besides a few scammers that will try and cheat the system regardless)? Hampton Inn is certainly putting their money where their mouth is!

---

34. http://hamptoninn3.hilton.com/en/about/index.html

HEALTHIER FOOD IS OUR PROMISE

Panera Bread is known for their freshness and commitment to serving "better for you" products including a multitude of salads, soups, sides, and breakfast items that won't break the bank or your waistline. Panera became so bold as of 2015 that they set a goal of removing all artificial preservatives, coloring, sweeteners or artificial flavors in their food by the end of 2016. Time will tell as to whether this guarantee is fully manifested but the fact that Panera has publicly proclaimed their "clean food journey" and listed over 70 different ingredients on their "No No List"[35] shows that they're serious about helping keep their customer's minds at ease and earn their complete trust.

BLINKING LIGHT? WE'LL MAKE IT RIGHT

Most would say that Sheetz is a gas station/convenience store, but Sheetz defines themselves as, "An American restaurant company with a focus on kicked-up convenience." One of Sheetz's differentiators is their promise to buy a cup of coffee for any guest that sees a blinking light on one of their coffee brewers (signifying that the coffee needs to be changed). This tactic is brilliant since consumers know that without the blinking light that the coffee is of the highest quality and that if they do happen to see a blinking light, that a freshly brewed cup will be offered to them on the house. This is a brilliant marketing strategy and a solid guarantee that helps sets Sheetz apart from the competition.

CHANGE FEE? NOT ON OUR WATCH

Anyone that has ever had a conflict in their calendar or had unforeseen circumstances arise knows how painful rescheduling a flight can be. Imagine your grandmother unexpectedly passing away and

---

35. https://www.panerabread.com/panerabread/documents/panera-no-no-list-05-2015.pdf

having to pay a $150 "change fee" because you have to attend a funeral. That's highway robbery (or skyway in this case) in our opinions. That's one of the very reasons why Southwest instituted their "no change fees" on all equal or lesser valued flights. According to Southwest:

> In today's fast-paced world, things can change in a moment's notice. That's why here at Southwest Airlines we continue to offer maximum flexibility if you need to modify your travel plans, by not charging change fees. If you need to change an upcoming flight itinerary, you'll only pay the cost in fare difference and will never incur a separate change fee. We don't charge you for changing your mind, your plans, or otherwise. So you can rest assured when booking your next Southwest Airlines flight that change fees don't fly with us.

That one simple guarantee is one of the pillars of the Southwest empire and helps put people's minds at ease. If you're able to change a flight without having to pay for a new one, that's a promise that's worth paying just a bit more for, isn't it?

YOU'LL LOVE DESSERT OR IT'S FREE

Cactus Restaurants, a chain located in Washington state, has a unique offer that they advertise. Cactus feels so confident in many of their desserts that they offer a money back guarantee. This is how Cactus describes their Three Milk Cuban Flan, "So good it comes with a money back guarantee."

It's simple but effective promise to Cactus guests. Besides, who in their right mind would return a dessert? When we asked if anyone has ever returned their signature dessert, one manager commented, "Never. Not a one."

THE ROCK SAID SO

When venturing to a Stew Leonard's grocery store and restaurant, one cannot walk in without seeing the three-ton boulder directly adjacent to the front door. Upon further examination, it's easy to see that Stew Leonard's make a rock solid guarantee to put consumer minds at ease (pardon the terrible pun). According to stew-leonards.com:

> On his way to work one morning, Stew drove by a monument yard, where they were unloading granite. Suddenly, Stew got an idea. He stopped and bought a huge slab of granite from Mr. Bates. It weighed 6,000 pounds. Then, Stew, had him deliver the rock to the front door of his store, and had their stonemason chisel the store's new policy into its face:
>
> **Rule 1:** The Customer Is Always Right!
>
> **Rule 2:** If The Customer Is Ever Wrong, Reread Rule 1.
>
> To this day, 35 years later, the rock still stands firm at each of Stew Leonard's store entrances... They know that they can do anything in their power to make the customer happy. Happy customers not only come back, they bring their friends!

As you can see, a strong guarantee not only makes the customers feel empowered, but the principle also transcends amongst the company's employees. If the guarantee is so remarkable, such as Stew Leonard's, then the story begins to spread to all of the stakeholders and the network attached to them.

20 MINUTES OR IT'S FREE

Judging from the headline, you would think that we're alluding to a guarantee similar to what Domino's built their empire on, "30 minutes or it's free." As an interesting side note, Domino's had to get rid of this promise as drivers got into a significant amount of accidents and it caused a safety hazard. However, we're not talking about this infamous guarantee; we're referencing the airline industry.

Let's be frank, getting your luggage at the airport is always a hassle. Even worse, are airline carriers notorious for how effective they are in delivering your valuables or famous for its ability to lose them? The latter is, unfortunately, the negative stereotype most commonly associated with airports. That's why Delta chose to up their game and offer the get your luggage to you in 20 minutes or less. According to Delta.com:

> We're committed to providing you with reliable and on-time baggage service every time you fly. That's why we're backing your bags with a guarantee: if your checked bag doesn't arrive at the carousel in 20 minutes or less after any domestic flight, you are eligible to receive 2,500 bonus miles. Just complete the below form no later than three days after your flight's arrival. Requests should only be submitted after your flight.

CHAPTER 17

#6 - PAY IT FORWARD

"One of the deep secrets of life is that all that is really worth doing is what we do for others."

—Lewis Carroll

GIVING BACK AND PAYING IT FORWARD

Sometimes the little extra is not about the customer, but rather giving back to the community or to those in need.

SIGNATURE LAGNIAPPE: ROSA'S FRESH PIZZA

Former financial associate, Mason Wartman, quit his dream Wall Street job to sell pizza in his hometown of Philadelphia. Wartman started Rosa's Fresh Pizza and had a simple idea one day of serving slices for just a buck and offering his customers to purchase a sticky note for another dollar and being able to place it on the wall of the restaurant. The sticky note can be redeemed by the homeless and entitles them to a free slice. The movement has become known as "pay it forward pizza" and the entire pizza shop is now filled with written responses of gratitude. How many sticky notes are there exactly? NPR recently reported that over 8,400 slices were purchased for future redemptions over nine months in 2014-2015.

According to Wartman, "This is a super-easy way, a super-efficient way and a super-transparent way to help the homeless. Sometimes homeless people buy [slices] for other homeless people." Not only are the good people of Rosa's helping combat the homeless epidemic but they're garnering national attention for the selfless move and were even given a surprise visit by Ellen Degeneres, who offered Wartman a $10,000 check to his cause. All of that positive publicity from such a simple "pay it forward" idea.

A TRAVEL COMPANION THAT HELPS THE COMMUNITY

At the Residence Inn in Mesa, AZ, they have instituted a "rent a fish" program (very similar to that of Kimpton's "Guppy Love"). The Residence Inn allows its guests to rent a beta fish for $5 per night or $20 per stay, and all of the proceeds go to the Phoenix Children's Hospital, Ronald McDonald House or another child-oriented charity that is chosen as the "charity of the month." Not only are guests kept company by the fish but their "rental fee" goes to good use in the community. A cool twist on one of our favorite "fish" programs!

A KITCHEN FOR THE NEEDY

Jim Noble is an accomplished restaurateur, but he felt a higher calling. Noble wanted to create a restaurant that did more than just serve exquisite food and bring friends and family closer together. What Noble set out to do was to create a restaurant where he could virtually eliminate homelessness in Charlotte, NC, and his project became known as King's Kitchen. How has he done it? Here are just a few features at King's Kitchen:

- All of the employees are considered "unhirable" by most societal norms. Noble teaches his employees soft skills and sets a goal of getting them a full-time job.

- King's Kitchen regularly feeds hundreds of homeless people on a weekly basis, and a portion of their proceeds go to various homeless initiatives throughout Charlotte.

- Noble often provides food and other resources for disaster relief in poverty stricken areas.

When asked about his inspiration to start the restaurant, Noble said, "The inspiration for The King's Kitchen — or marching orders, as Noble puts it — comes from the Bible. We have to do it. It's like when you're in the Army. If you wake up and don't make your bed, you get into trouble. We have to feed the poor."

RANDOM ACTS OF KINDNESS SERVED PRETTY DARN QUICK

Tampa-based fast-casual chicken chain, PDQ, has gone out of their way to create a whole day of random acts of kindness. The chain designates one day in February where customers are selected (without notice) to have their entire meal comped. There's no catch to receive the offer either. It's simply a meal on the house to pay it forward for others.

According to operating director, Tommy Hintzman, in The Villages, FL, "Our company-wide goal was to give at least three meals per hour, but once you started giving, it became a lot of fun. When you think about the 50 units all giving at this rate for the entire day; that's a lot of 'feel good' chicken!"

HONORING THOSE THAT PROTECT US

Business partners, Steve "Newt" Newton and Bill Kraus, set out to create a chain of barbecue restaurants that not only served top-notch food but also stood for something much deeper. Newt and Kraus ended up landing on a mission to reward the public service sector for their protection and aptly named the restaurant, Mission BBQ. Mission defines their purpose as:

> To support our local police, fire departments, and armed services, Mission collects donations and constantly holds special events. This has allowed Mission to raise tens of thousands of dollars for numerous noteworthy causes and organizations, including the Wounded Warrior Project, the USO, and Toys for Tots.

Bill Krause elaborated on the mission by saying, "Our mission at Mission BBQ is to serve. The world didn't need another restaurant, but maybe it needed a place that stands for what's right, and that makes you feel good if you have served or are serving." Kudos to you, Mission BBQ!

FLY IT FORWARD

JetBlue introduced its latest promotional effort, a campaign called "Fly It Forward" that provides consumers worthy of admiration with a free flight and gives them the chance to do the same for others. The project kicked off with a Chicago community worker-turned-United Nations delegate who received a ticket to New York City. She, in turn, awarded one to a woman who was in rehab after losing both her legs in an accident, and the trend continued. JetBlue launched the campaign with four profiles selected by JetBlue crew members and a planning team that "scoured the social web for deserving stories." Then it turned the job over to the people of Twitter, asking them to nominate "Fly It Forward" candidates.

> "These aren't intended to be marketing stories or Jet-Blue stories," Marty St. George, JetBlue's senior vice president of commercial, says. "These are customer stories that illustrate the impact that travel can have to make dreams come true." With its continuous stream of compassionate video content and serialized story-telling, #FlyItForward has generated 1,192 posts and nominations to date. Twitter users are calling it "a beautiful idea," and an "awesome way of awarding humanitarian efforts to those who deserve it." According to the company, there's no campaign end date in sight.

#DAYOFGIVING

Jersey Mike's Subs, known for its freshly prepared submarine sandwiches, asks customers to eat a sub and help a local charity during the month of March every year which they call the "Month of Giving." The 2015 "Month of Giving" raised more than $3 million for more than 150 different charities nationwide and Jersey Mike's has plans to break this record year after year. As of 2016, Jersey Mike's has created a national event, known as a #dayofgiving (the hashtag was included to help promote social media conversations) where 100 percent of the day's sales are donated to a local partner charity.

Peter Cancro, Jersey Mike's founder, commented on the #dayofgiving initiative by saying, "This year, as we celebrate 60 years in business, we hope to raise more than $3.5 million to help local charities. It's gratifying to know that each new location brings more opportunities to make a difference in people's lives."

CHAPTER 18

#7 - FOLLOW-UP

"Learn to say thank you every time."

—Jill Griff

FOLLOWING UP AND SAYING "THANK YOU"

A fter covering six "value" PGs, this chapter marks the first type of "maintenance" focused Purple Goldfish. The seventh Purple Goldfish is the expression of gratitude to a customer. A personal gesture that conveys both appreciation and acknowledgment.

SIGNATURE LAGNIAPPE: WINE LIBRARY

Gary Vaynerchuk is the outspoken former owner of a huge wine retailer, Wine Library. Along the way, Gary discovered the importance of engaging customers before there were problems to prevent damage control and proactively build relationships. This led to the creation of a department aptly named, "The Thank You Department" whose responsibilities including contacting every single customer and thanking them for their business. No upsell, no cross-sell, and no agenda in mind. Wine Library was genuinely vested in showing their gratitude toward the people that paid their bills.

In an interview with Gary Vaynerchuk, Nick Francis of Helpscout. com, uncovered the following about the "Thank You Department":

> I did it because I...thought it would be a good idea. The other reason I did it was I just thought there'd be a lot of value to it. I think of customer service as an offense and not a defense. I just believe that giving is always the right thing and so that's why I'm doing it.
>
> Saying thank you and putting a piece of chocolate in a bottle of wine shipment, writing a handwritten letter, replying to people on Twitter and Facebook, doing data research on people that are great customers that we haven't said hello to in a while and just calling them

and saying thank you for no reason whatsoever. Those things add up, and I think that they really matter.

THANK YOU FOR LETTING US SERVE

The restaurant chain, Mission BBQ, did not set out to create more than two restaurants back in 2011, but as of 2016, there are over 30 locations, and they are still growing. The reason for this success is predominantly because of Mission's culture and abundant giving.

According to Mission's National Community Ambassador, Kerry Johnston:

> We spend no money on traditional advertising and choose to use our marketing dollars to serve our community. A lot of our budget is spent on our community ambassadors taking food to the police, fire departments, and first responders that serve in the areas where our restaurants are. We give without expecting anything in return and always write hand-written thank you notes to the respective public service groups.

Lagniappe Takeaway: Mission is doing what is right in their minds and going above to thank our public service sector for being able to donate food for them. This is not an aspect that Mission freely talks about either. Somehow the word about this abundant gratitude and thankfulness still manages to get around.

GRATITUDE IN ANY LANGUAGE

The Residence Frond Neige in Morzine, France, makes it a habit of thanking its guests quickly and professionally across online review sites. What's even more impressive about what the Frond Neige team does is how genuine the responses are. Many hospitality institutions automate their responses or choose to hire a third party to provide the same canned answers over and over again.

A guest from England left this review on TripAdvisor:

> We stayed during the early season in the summer (July 2015) the weather was very hot, but with the fantastic breeze and shutters that were in the room made it very easy and relaxing in the room. The location was perfect with amazing views and easy access to the lovely town of Morzine. Eric, Ann-laure, and Elina were the perfect hosts. Every evening we would watch as the paragliders would descend from Avoriaz and land outside the room.

Though English is not the ownership's primary language, the owners still responded, "We are so glad you liked your stay with us. We hope next time, the weather will be a little cooler so that we can show you some of the nicest walks around the region. We hope to see you again soon!"

Let's review the keys to why Frond Neige's "thank you" is so remarkable:

- **All reviews are equal** - Frond Neige responds to all reviews whether they are positive or negative. Most establishments only try to do damage control and are not proactive with their gratitude and customer relationship building.

- **Speed** - All of Frond Neige's replies happen the same day. The fact that Frond Neige makes this a daily practice to respond to reviews tells you the importance of this activity in their minds.

- **Genuity** - Frond Neige takes the time to read the review and addresses the specific points that are made.

THE CAPTAIN'S PERSONAL TOUCH

Taken from a blog post at ivanmisner.com:

Long lines, deteriorating service, flight attendants grabbing a beer and pulling the emergency exit handle to slide out onto the tarmac are part of our vision of airlines these days. However, I had an experience last week that was amazing in this day and age. My wife and I were flying on United from LAX to New Orleans for a business conference. Before we were about to land, Rebecca, the flight attendant, handed me a business card from the Captain. His name is Patrick Fletcher. On the back of Captain Fletcher's card was a handwritten note that said:

Mr. and Mrs. Misner,

It's great to have you both with us today – Welcome! I hope you have a great visit to New Orleans – we really appreciate your business!

Sincerely, Pat Fletcher

Rebecca (who was a great flight attendant, by the way), told me the Captain wrote these notes to everyone who was a member of their premier-level frequent flier club as well as all the first class passengers. On this day, that was around 12 people. She said he is great to fly with because he really treats the passengers AND the crew very well, mentioning that he had brought scones to all of them that morning.

I fly A LOT. In the last 20 years, I've probably traveled on over 800 flights all around the world. In that time, I have never received a personal note from the

Captain. Entrepreneurs and major corporations alike can learn from this story. Personal service that goes above and beyond the call of duty can generate great word of mouth.

Captain Fletcher – my hat's off to you. Well done. I think this is a great example of how one person in a really large company can make a difference in a customer's attitude. Your note was creative and appreciated. I hope to be flying with you again.

WRITE THEM A NOTE...THEY'VE EARNED IT

José Pinto, the general manager of Le Mèridien restaurant in Dubai, does not take positive reviews lightly. In fact, Pinto is proactive and takes the time to type up a note recognizing everything that a reviewer has done for the restaurant. Take this example from a note that Jose wrote to a guest:

> We appreciated you liking and posting on our Facebook page. We're even more grateful to have seen and read your views about our experience on your blog. It boosts the morale of the staff and makes a positive impression for our current and future guests..
>
> Thank you again for taking the time to write about your experiences...we are grateful for your support.

Food bloggers, food writers, Yelpers, and social media power users are incessantly asked to visit restaurants so that the establishment can leverage their name and reputation. The part that most hospitality folks forget is that these people are taking their precious time to give and rarely ever provided anything past a plate of food and an expectation. Kudos to Pinto and the Le Mèridien restaurant for taking the time to recognize their key folks!

AN ARTISAN DESSERT FOR YOUR SERVICE

An hourly kitchen employee at the Montage Hotel in Laguna Beach, CA, started making waves when he began customizing complimentary desserts for guests that he enjoyed. According to a thread on Imgur.com, the expediter has one special example:

> A guy was sporting a Navy SEAL Trident hat, so we got to talking. It turns out that his brother-in-law has a foundation for Navy SEAL wives who have lost their husbands in combat. It started to rain, and he left in haste (not knowing I was working on this one), so I didn't quite finish the details so I could try and find him in the lobby. He wound up writing a letter to my GM; I was given a free dinner at the restaurant and money was donated to the Navy SEAL foundation in my name. Pretty happy about that!

When examining this anecdote, we see an hourly team member was allowed the autonomy to comp a dessert, elegantly design the plate, and had enough foresight to thank a member of our armed forces. If that isn't a cool "thank you gift" and tremendous empowerment of the hourly staff then we don't know what is!

A THANK YOU TO OUR NEIGHBORS

Comfort Suites in Mount Pleasant, SC, decided to say "thank you" to all of their neighbors in a very interesting way. The Comfort Suites sent out invitations to a significant amount of their neighboring businesses to come and enjoy the Comfort brand's free signature waffles on National Waffle Day. According to the Moultrie News:

> "Although we are in the travel business, the Comfort brand also has strong roots in the local communities we serve," said Anne Smith, vice president of brand

strategy for Choice Hotels International. "This iconic brand has had incredible staying power because we understand the importance of doing more than just setting up shop in a town. Going above and beyond is the essence of Comfort hospitality and our franchisees are excited to express their appreciation."

Comfort Suites illustrates a strong point. A lot of times companies get so fixated on serving their customers that they forget to show appreciation for their neighbors and greater communities that they operate in. Know who your neighbors and general community is made up of? You guessed it. Your customers! Big props to Comfort Suites for sharing some syrupy love to show their gratitude.

THANK YOU ON VIDEO

British Airways decided to express their gratitude over the 2015 winter holidays by involving the fans in "thank you" social media content pieces. The first of which being a video that features pictures submitted by the fans on the airline and expanding into a bigger campaign from there. According to the Content Marketing Association:

> A video thanking flyers for traveling with British Airways launched on December 1st that features a series of UGC [user generated content] holiday snaps to recognize the incredible journeys that passengers have embarked on this year. British Airways is to communicate a seasonal 'thank-you' message to passengers this Christmas by way of a two-way conversation on social media in which the airline will express its gratitude to customers for choosing the flag carrier.

Incorporating a 70-second video clip produced by Cedar the campaign features images sent in by travelers and will be distributed across Facebook, Instagram, Twitter, and Google + as well as the airline's in-flight entertainment system. A competition will run in parallel with this effort inviting people to submit Instagram images recommending destinations to others for 2015.

Abigail Comber, British Airways' head of global marketing, said, "Our customers are some of the world's greatest travelers and explorers, and featuring them at the heart of this campaign is just our way of saying a really big thank-you for sharing those experiences with us this year. They've sent in all sorts of images from once-in-a-lifetime parachute jumps to visits to great global sites like the Taj Mahal. "We can't wait to see where our customers want to head to in 2016 and are looking forward to being a part of their incredible journeys."

KNOW YOUR CUSTOMER

Marty Desmond left this example within a comment on Kelly Ketelboeter's post, "What is Your Purple Goldfish?" This is how Marty describes Gumba's in Sunnyvale, CA:

> I went for breakfast with friends at one of our favorite places on Saturday. We sat outdoors for the first time since street construction began months ago. As we were served, I watched how much fun the employees were having. I told my friends that it was great seeing the restaurant busy again and that I knew the construction hurt much of the business on that block.

I went back Tuesday evening for a quick dinner. As I was eating, the owner came up, patted me on the back and thanked me for my business Saturday morning. Then, he told me how happy he was to see my friends and inquired about them. He asked if the dad had found another job, knowing that he was laid off months ago.

We talked for a few moments more, and then he patted me on the back again, thanked me once more and walked off. I watched him walk away and thought about why I enjoyed that restaurant so much. The food is great, but it's the experience that makes it worth going back.

I realize that no fewer than four of his employees approached my friend to tell them how much they had missed his family. The culture of that business includes personal relationships whenever possible. I think that is a missing ingredient in so many businesses today.

This restaurant has endured six months of lagging sales, due to people wanting to stay away during construction. Regardless, they were genuinely concerned about the lives of the people who walked through their doors. To me, every question of "how is your friend" is a Purple Goldfish.

CHAPTER 19

#8 - ADDED SERVICE

"It has long been an axiom of mine that the little things are infinitely the most important."

—Sir Arthur Conan Doyle

AN ADDED TOUCH FOR GOOD MEASURE

The eighth of the 12 types of Purple Goldfish is an "added service." In essence, a little extra service that exceeds the expectations of your customers.

SIGNATURE LAGNIAPPE: HOTEL DRISCO

Reader, Evan Hoffman, had this to say about Hotel Drisco in San Francisco, CA:

> Easily the most memorable hotel stay of my life. Drisco had all of what you would expect regarding amenities, service, and overall experience for over $300 per night. However, all of the extra services that they provide make it an experience worth sharing with everyone that you know. Hats off to Hotel Drisco!

After reviewing hoteldrisco.com,[36] we assembled a top 10 of complimentary services that Hotel Drisco offers their guests:

1. Complimentary use of the nearby Presidio YMCA fitness center

2. Evening wine reception with artisan cheeses, charcuterie, fruit and a hot hors d'oeuvre

3. Morning newspaper delivered to your room

4. Coffee and tea available 24 hours a day in the Sitting Room with handmade biscotti served at 3:00 PM

5. Overnight shoeshine service

6. Weekday morning chauffeur service to select destinations

---

36. http://www.hoteldrisco.com/hotel-services/san-Francisco-boutique-hotels

7. Six bicycles complete with helmets, locks, backpacks and water bottles

8. Use your guestroom phone to make complimentary calls anywhere in the continental United States

9. Plentiful street parking available. Unlike downtown hotels where parking fees can exceed $50 per night, on-street parking at Hotel Drisco is free and convenient.

10. A small business center on our ground floor with a powerful big-screen PC, blazing fast Internet access, a full suite of Microsoft Office Programs, a laser printer, business tools, basic office supplies, and a speakerphone with toll-free calling to anywhere in the continental United States. You need not reserve this space in advance, but you may if you wish. All of this is complimentary, of course.

AN UNEXPECTED BOOK

World traveling blogger and photographer, Jen Pollack Bianco, visited the Sheraton Bratislava in Slovakia and never expected to find the gift that she came across. According to Bianco:

> After a long day of travel via Zurich and Vienna, I finally arrived at the Sheraton Bratislava. Waiting for me in Suite 717 was a book of Instagram Moments with a note from the staff that said, "As we know that Jennifer loves to take Instagram pictures, we thought you'd enjoy this hand-picked selection of 25 of our most favorite shots of Bratislava...;)"

> Starwood has always been a social media savvy brand, and this is just more proof of why. The book is printed

rather nicely and will serve as a visual guide book during my stay here.

Bianco promptly took photos of the book and wrote a blog entry on her site, lifesatrip.com, about the experience to her huge, dedicated audience. Perhaps this move risks coming off as contrived but because of the willingness to help Bianco without looking for anything in return (such as asking for a review), the Sheraton scored major brownie points in the social media and photography worlds.

LOTS OF GREAT STEAKS IN TOWN, ONE ANGUS BARN

Alyssa Barkley, of the North Carolina Restaurant & Lodging Association, offered this gem about Van Eure, the owner of the Angus Barn in Raleigh, NC:

> Van will be the first to tell you that there are many comparable products in town and she'll even give you directions and make recommendations as to what dishes to get. However, Eure emphasizes that guests come to the Angus Barn when they want an unforgettable experience. If all hands are on deck and the team is committed to the same goal; it's hard not to create a different experience.

In this example, it's apparent that Eure believes in abundance. Van graciously shares business with her competitors and surprises her current and potential guests with the added service of making favorable recommendations.

LET'S START WITH PURPOSE

John Rivers was a medical executive in Winter Park, FL, that identified an opportunity to share his world renowned brisket recipe to help make the world a better place. John first utilized his brisket in a barbecue fundraiser to raise money for a neighborhood child with cancer. John then used his barbecue as a Christian-based catering vehicle aimed at bettering the community. Eventually, John's operation got so famous that he felt the need to build one fast casual restaurant which is now known as 4Rivers Smokehouse.

4Rivers serves the community in multiple ways, yet it's their commitment to establishing guest needs that sets them apart. 4Rivers staff are encouraged to proactively find different ways to service their guests and offer them additional services. According to John:

> Every aspect of our restaurant is tailored to create an experience, from our staff to our facility. At 4Rivers, we know that from the moment guests pull into our store or call in an order, the precedence is set for our team to exceed their expectations. Our team members are encouraged to actively engage guest's needs with a relationship mindset, rather than a task-oriented focus. Yes, we sell food, although we have never considered ourselves to be solely in the food industry. Instead, our success has been derived from our business approach as a provider of experiences and our team's ability to bring that approach to life.

WHAT ELSE CAN WE DO?
THE SOCIAL WEB WILL KNOW

According to Nancy Trejos at USA Today, Accor Hotels implemented a program that identified loyalty members checking into the hotels that month, and then matched the guests to their social media profiles. Accor used this data to determine the interests of their guests at its Sofitel and Novotel properties throughout the United States. Magali Jimenez Berville, director of e-commerce North America for Accor, commented that this program would, "Take guest recognition to the next level, to a more powerful level." What were the net results? Guests received the following:

- One guest talked exclusively about fine dining and was provided an all-day behind-the-scenes tour of Tru restaurant in Chicago along with a night at the Sofitel Chicago Water Tower.

- Another guest often emphasized their love of fishing and was provided an eco-friendly fishing trip in the San Diego Bay.

- Another guest commented on luxury cars and was given a certificate to drive Ferrari and Lamborghini automobiles.

- Finally, a guest that emphasized their love of sports was provided VIP tickets to a hockey game between the San Jose Sharks and the Red Wings.

ALLOW US TO CREATE YOU A "YOUTILITY"

Jay Baer, a *New York Times* best-selling author recently wrote a book called *Youtility*. The premise of the book is simple; Jay believes that smart marketing is about helping the people that you serve what than hype (i.e. pitching them with advertising). One of Jay's favorite examples of a company that provides an added service that genuinely helps the masses comes from Hilton. Hilton created a Twitter account, @HiltonSuggests, that monitors Twitter and answers questions that travelers have about cities they are going to that they are unfamiliar with. Expion, who recently hosted Jay as a keynote speaker at their annual conference, had this to add:

The objective of *Youtility* is not just making information – it's about making information that customers and prospects find useful. In fact, so useful that they would pay for it and of course, tell their friends about it. Always keep in mind that you are answering the following question, "How can we help you be more awesome?" For @HiltonSuggests, that infused awesomeness is helping their customers and prospects find the perfect Sports Bar in Tampa, the best golf course in Nashville or a restaurant with a great view in Chicago.

Even though you might not be staying with Hilton in the city that you're visiting, you know that they provide a useful added service where you can find exactly what you're looking for in a new city. Now, the next time that you're given the option of staying at a Hilton or with another hotel, Hilton will typically win because of the added service that they've provided you in the past.

IT'S IN THE NAME

When your restaurant is called "Above and Beyond" then one would hope that you would never disappoint. In fact, Above and Beyond, in Hong Kong lives up to and, you guessed it, surpasses its namesake. According to one reviewer from TripAdvisor:

> As a westerner, my palate for authentic Chinese dining is still developing, and I have sometimes struggled with ordering. The menu at Above and Beyond had a broad selection and did not disappoint at all. What a wonderful meal. Although there are several house specialities, we went for one of the set menus and had course after course of delicious fare. The views were spectacular (we booked in advance and managed to get

a table at the window). This is a wonderful, trendy yet romantic setting.

The service was impeccable! Surreptitious and discreet, but always prompt. We need to make special mention of two gentlemen who greatly assisted in our enjoyment of the evening. Assistant manager Bill Yau made several recommendations and ensured that our dining experience was flawless. He even gave us a parting gift of tea and biscuits as we were too full to complete our meal with tea. Sommelier Wallace Lo was extremely knowledgeable and paired the perfect wines for the set menu, not always an easy feat with so many courses. This is a pricey night out, but not unreasonably so. The quality of the food, service and location justify the cost, and we would return again when next in Hong Kong.

Extra Lagniappe: On top of the full service and additional gift, the reviewer also received the wines to complement the dishes on the house as well. Talk about going the extra mile to provide exemplary service!

FAST, CASUAL, AND NOW HIGH TOUCH

This example comes courtesy of Jennifer Phelps. In Jenn's words, "Boston Market gives kids balloons (which is nice). They also carry your tray to your table which is helpful." Boston Market turned 30 years old in 2015. It looks like they are revamping both their offerings and service model. According to seriouseats.com:

Boston Market is giving its restaurants something of a makeover. 370 of their nearly 500 locations will be revamped by the end of 2010, with the stores in the Miami and New York markets leading the charge. Some of the changes are small; some are large. The side orders in the "Hot Case" will be cooked in smaller pots, so the food is prepared more frequently, and less is wasted. They are increasing staff, and will have employees escorting customers to their tables, as well as bussing the tables after they're finished. Finally, and most interestingly, Boston Market is introducing real plates and silverware for dine-in guests—bringing the experience away from the traditional tray-to-table fast-food model.

The renovations can be summed up by Tony Buford, Senior Vice President – Operations at Boston Market, "We are proud of our new offering but it's more than just paint, pots, and poultry – it's the people. The people are the heart and soul of the company, and what makes Boston Market America's kitchen table." Kudos to Boston Market for raising their game and focusing on customer experience.

SMALL BUT VALUABLE

Submitted by Brian Millman:

Porter Airlines is a short-haul airline which flies out of Toronto's City Centre airport (very cute and small airport) and focuses on business travelers. It started primarily operating in Canada with one US route to Newark but has expanded to fly to Boston, Chicago, and Myrtle Beach. With most airlines, you expect to sit in the typical terminal with old rows of seats. At Porter's hub, they offer a VIP lounge for everyone. The terminal area is set up similar to that of any VIP lounge: a kitchen stocked filled with free soda and water, two cappuccino machines, and free snacks (cookies and chips).

Porter also offers free Wi-Fi with a power port under every seat as well as 14 computers for those without a laptop. Finally, I'm not sure if I have gotten lucky, but supposedly there is a $100 change fee for jumping on an earlier flight, but I haven't been charged for it once.

WAIT, YOU CAN DO SOMETHING?

How many times have you been to a restaurant where your order was wrong or something was unsatisfactory about your meal? Probably more than you care to admit. Who was it that ultimately dealt with the situation? Perhaps the manager if you can find them? How does it make sense to put the burden on you as a consumer to track down the person/people in the building that can render your problem? To change this formula around, pizza chain Fazoli's took action. This excerpt comes from an article in QSR magazine by Marlee Murphy:

> When the economy began recovering from the 2008 recession, Italian [quick serve] chain Fazoli's decided to add service beyond the point of sale. CEO Carl Howard says it was one of the best decisions the brand has ever made. According to Howard, "My philosophy has always been that I could win on two qualities: service and hospitality," he says. "Foodservice and hospitality will be able to earn market share from my competitors and also give me pricing elasticity moving forward."
>
> Howard has led Fazoli's transformation over the past few years into a more service-oriented brand. The staff now brings food to the guests' tables and has

an employee dedicated to breadstick duty, providing guests with bread and other services. To help establish best-in-class service, Howard says, the brand is in the process of yet another service initiative by adding a "guest ambassador"—the senior-most manager on duty who will be in the dining room instead of behind the counter.

Props to Fazoli's for stepping up their game. Allocating resources to include rarely provided services in their industry was a huge move for their integrity, and it also helped their top line.

DISNEY BRIGHTENS YOUR DAY

According to our friend, and Disney college intern, Hailie Williams:

> We guest service like nobody's business on every shift we have. We usually try to read into conversations and turn the guests day around so we offer them complimentary buttons to celebrate birthdays, graduations, happily ever afters, etc. One thing that's really cool is we're given a phone number though the company's line, and it's Goofy who wishes the guest a happy birthday. If we see the button, we don't even ask sometimes we just dial the number and say they have a phone call or someone wants to tell them something.

> Disney has mastered the art. It's really awesome because our whole purpose is to make the guest happy, so we are as courteous as possible. It's one of our keys.

We don't know about you, but if we got a button and a call from Goofy, we'd say that those additional services would make your special day just a little more memorable!

PUT IT IN THE COOP

Chick-fil-A is known for its focus on customer service and receives higher marks than any other fast food chain (and it's not even close). One new initiative encourages family interaction and rewards their guests for doing so. The restaurant places a small, square box, (AKA "the Coop") on each table, with a simple challenge: enjoy a meal without the distraction of cellphones. Guests complete the challenge successfully only if cell phones remain in the Coop untouched for their entire meal. According to Brad Williams, the Suwanee, GA, Chick-fil-A operator that started the initiative:

> I've been doing this for 25 years and, over that time, I've seen customers at our restaurant go from spending quality time and talking with one another to being on their phones the entire meal. There's just a major disconnect. The challenge has completely taken off. We have families who don't make it the first time, either because they ended up texting or something else, but then they come back in to try it again. Now we even have people asking to take the boxes home with them!

The program has been such a hit that Chick-fil-A units all over the country are embracing the challenge. Not only is Chick-fil-A bringing families closer together but they also reward their guests with an ice cream cone as a sweet surprise. Chick-fil-A is certainly going the extra mile to ensure that their guests have an even better than usual experience.

CHAPTER 20

#9 - WAITING

*"The secret to success is to treat all customers as if
your world revolves around them."*

—Unknown

WE SPEND TEN PERCENT OF LIFE WAITING

The 9th of the 12 types of Purple Goldfish is all about "waiting." Your customers having to wait is inevitable, especially if you are a successful business. How you handle those moments, and the little extras you offer can make a big difference.

SIGNATURE LAGNIAPPE: DISNEY

Disney knows that because of its popularity that there will be times when families have to wait at its theme parks, restaurants, and lodging. That's not always the best combination when there are children involved and it's the very reason Disney developed "Disney Inquizitive." The Disney app has thousands of quizzes about its movies, TV shows, characters, Walt Disney himself, and much more. What may seem like a drag on the overall Disney experience has now been transformed into a fun game that allows the family to play along.

That's just one example. The fact is, when you go to Disney, you're anticipating on waiting a lot. For that reason, Disney spends an inordinate time creating "Interaction Queues" to entertain you while you wait. Here's an example from T.J. Van Fetchmann over at touringplans.com:

> I do not like waiting in lines. I'm an impatient person, and I always have been. But I do love Disney World so you can see how this could be a problem for me. Thankfully, Disney is all about making every experience at their parks magical. Yup, even the waiting in long lines part. Over the past several years, I've noticed a trend at Disney Parks where many attraction queues have been getting special care and attention to become more immersive and interactive. Of course, not

all lines, waiting areas, and queues are created equal. Some attraction queues are done so well that they feel like a natural extension of the attraction itself while others are indistinguishable from waiting in line at the bank only if the bank were outside in 90-degree weather and the customers all wore fanny packs and mouse ears.

If Disney gave out Most Improved Awards, the queue for Peter Pan's Flight...would most certainly be a frontrunner. Before the refurbishment, guests simply had to wait in a long line that practically extended into Liberty Square. It's still a long line, but you'll now get to walk through the Darling children's nursery with plenty of effects and interactive elements that kids will love. The new queue effectively extends the entire experience and arguably becomes a part of the attraction, which is a trend that I don't expect Disney to stop anytime soon. Good job, Imagineers.

SAFETY IS IMPORTANT...NOW LAUGH

This example comes from our good friend, David Rendall, that offered the following, "I love Delta's safety video. Entertainment in the place of boredom. Surprising and delightful." What Dave is referencing is a mandatory safety video that Delta plays for passengers before taking off. As Mike Dunphy of roadwarriorvoices.com puts it:

> Experienced fliers usually tune out pre-flight safety videos with a "seen-one-seen-'em-all" attitude (guilty). Instead, we take the moment as our last chance to update Facebook before free Internet disappears. That's

why airlines are turning to humor in an attempt to get passengers to pay attention.

The newest in a series of comical safety videos comes from Delta, which continues the wacky humor of its previous videos with this Family Guy-like blend of instructions and goofy cut-aways, that features a giant squirrel fitting a nut in the overhead bin, the creatures of Yo Gabba Gabba doing the Harlem Shake, and — wait for it — Moses parting the aisles.

LET US WAIT WITH YOU

This comes to us from reader, Rocco Romeo, about his recent experience at the iconic In-N-Out Burger:

> There's always a line at the counter at In-N-Out, so I decided to take my chances and try the drive-thru. Surprisingly, the drive-thru line didn't take that long and seemed to move faster than the counter service inside. I thought it was awesome that they had an employee walk to my car, hand me a menu, and talk me through how and what to order. Since I was the last car in line, she even talked to me while I waited which was awesome and helped pass the time. It only took about three minutes to pull up to the cashier where my food was already waiting for me.

> I was so impressed because In-N-Out made a conscious effort to reduce my wait time and help keep me company during the process on top of it. Can't say enough great things about them!

PEANUTS ARE A TASTY DIVERSION

As we mentioned before, Five Guys Burgers and Fries is one of our favorite waiting examples of a lagniappe. There is a huge box of lightly salted peanuts when you walk in. In the early days, the long lines forced Jerry Murrell and his sons to distribute free, unshelled peanuts to placate waiting customers. The peanuts have become a Five Guys trademark.

HAVE A GLASS ON US

Pacific Cafe, a seafood restaurant in San Francisco, CA, offers free glasses of wine while you wait for a table. They don't accept reservations and it's a popular spot, so the beverage is a nice gesture to extend to patrons as they wait to be seated.

DON'T BE AN IG-NO-RA-MOOSE

The restaurant chain, Cracker Barrel, has made a name for itself in the "waiting game" by offering plentiful wooden front porch seating including their signature rocking chairs. While this aspect certainly provides a more pleasant experience while your table is being prepared, there are two more factors that set Cracker Barrel apart. According to reader, Missy McCarty:

> Cracker Barrel is a haven for children. Between the golf tee game, tabletop checkers, and the gift shop, there's just so much for restless kids to do while they wait for the food to arrive. It's such a simple thing, but virtually no one else has simple games that challenge our children's minds rather than coloring with crayons where they're going to make a mess.

A HOTEL IN THE TERMINAL

Anyone that has spent significant time waiting at an airport can attest to how trying to catch up on some Z's in an airport terminal is highly uncomfortable. Plus, who wants to lay across a bunch of seats or lay on the dirty ground? That's where reader, Mike Thomas, offered his feedback about waiting at airports:

> I travel all over the world. My life is packed into a suitcase. With that sort of regimen, you're going to have layovers. With the longer ones, there's typically a complimentary shuttle to a nearby hotel; that's no big deal. But what do you do when you've got a short wait and just need some quiet to get some work done or just enjoy a comfortable, relaxing area?
>
> Airports and airlines don't have anything for frequent travelers to get ready to stay a while. That's until I came across the SnoozeCube in Dubai's airport. Brilliant. It's cheap, it's comfortable, and versatile. You can get work done, watch TV, sleep or do whatever else you need to do without going through the hassle of getting a hotel (which might not be practical anyhow). Talk about helping the time go by!

CNN.com went a step further and detailed the SnoozeCube:

> Situated in Terminal one of Dubai International Airport, SnoozeCube offers a compact and soundproof room complete with bed, touchscreen TV, and internet access. There are currently 10 units in operation and a one-hour stay costs as little as $16. All SnoozeCubes are connected to the airport's flight information system to ensure that passengers do not miss their flights.

MAY I HAVE A LAYOVER PLEASE?

Let's face it, no one wants to encounter a lengthy layover. It's a necessary evil in the airlines industry and one that not many carriers put an emphasis on regarding accommodations for its passengers. Some higher end airlines will provide snacks or even an overnight stay for its first class passengers, but that's typically the extent of their offering. Reader, Udit Chaudry, submitted this example, "Emirates gives you meal vouchers for use in Dubai airport for your layover. I believe that they offer this service for even the shortest layovers, and the program is for everyone on the plane, including the economy class."

The beauty of this initiative is that it includes all of the passengers on the plane, and there are no limitations so that passengers can enjoy the multitude of options at the Dubai airport. Well done, Emirates!

CHAPTER 21

#10 - CONVENIENCE

"We see our customers as invited guests
to a party, and we are the hosts.
It's our job every day to make every important aspect
of the customer experience a little bit better."

—Jeff Bezos

EASY PEASY...GEORGE AND WEEZY

The tenth of the 12 types of Purple Goldfish surrounds the idea of "convenience." A little unexpected extra that makes things easier.

SIGNATURE LAGNIAPPE: CHICK-FIL-A

Corralling up the little ones when going out to eat can prove to be tough. That's why fast-casual chicken giant, Chick-fil-A, instituted the "Parent's Valet." The parent's valet is an initiative where parents can go through the drive-thru to order their food and the Chick-fil-A team will set a table up inside with all of the food laid out already. This alleviates the pain that parents experience when trying to go through the counter ordering process while simultaneously trying to corral their children.

According to Chick-fil-A's vice president of menu strategy and development, David Farmer, "[Parent's Valet] is part of Chick-fil-A's renewed focus on "taking the stress out" and making its restaurants a more relaxing place for customers." A Chick-fil-A spokesperson recently spoke to Chris Fuhrmeister over at eater.com and added this:

> Parent's Valet started organically at one of our restaurants and has since grown to be available in approximately 100 of our 1,900-plus locations. Each restaurant decides whether to offer the program based on their individual traffic and customer needs, but of course, our goal is to provide exceptional service to all of our customers each and every day. Our hope is that with ongoing improvements to our mobile ordering app, all customers will have access to this level of convenience in all locations in the future.

WHY WASTE TIME? LET'S EAT!

Our good friend and mentor, Shep Hyken, offered this example:

> At the famous Italian restaurant, Il Mullino, the moment you sit down they start bringing you appetizers. This is part of the experience. No extra charge, but at their prices, it's built in. Still, the first time you go there you say, 'WOW!'

There's certainly something to be said for instant gratification and engaging the guest right away rather than drawing out the process with lengthy greetings and order taking. Well done, Il Mullino!

REDEFINING HOURS OF OPERATION

This example comes to us from Ari Weissman of uxmag.com. Ari says:

> In 1927, an entrepreneurial worker at the Southland Ice Company in Dallas, Texas, began selling milk, bread, and eggs from a storefront on the ice dock to make a little extra money. Having access to an inexhaustible amount of ice for preserving the groceries, Joe Thompson was able to sell when other local grocery stores were closed in the late evenings and on weekends. For the first time, the local community could shop outside of typical business hours, whenever it suited them. Soon after, Joe added gasoline and various other food, drinks, and "convenience" items to his inventory in a new store with the unprecedented trading hours of 7 a.m. to 11 p.m. By 2011, 7-Eleven has grown to 41,000 locations worldwide and is the prototype for convenience.

Tens of thousands of stores just because Thompson was willing to open a little earlier and stay open a little bit later to make life a bit more convenient. As a quick aside, 7-Eleven's corporate website as of 2016 states the chain now operates, franchises, and licenses over 56,600 units in over 18 countries with 10,500 being in North America.

NOT YOUR AVERAGE HOTEL

Airbnb has taken the world by storm by allowing virtually anyone to leave rooms or their entire home up for rent. Typically, it's for a fraction of the cost of a hotel and encompasses a feeling of "home away from home." The extra amenities and added services by the Airbnb hosts help the service differentiate itself further. According to frequent traveler and Airbnb host, Saurabh Chawla:

> As a host, I often leave detailed instructions and directions so that my guests can get around to the "must see" local spots. I always try to be present so that I can show people around the "must see" places without my guests having to look everything up on their own. To better serve people, we became the first licensed Airbnb in Colorado's third largest city. Busted my butt for seven months to get city council to make it happen!

CURBSIDE SERVICE MADE SIMPLE

Stan's friend, Jack Campisi, advocated the curbside approach at Thai Basil in Greenwich, CT. According to Jack:

> Thai Basil is most certainly a Purple Goldfish. Not only do they have great Thai food, but excellent service as well. Their lagniappe is the curbside pick-up. They are located on a busy and crowded stretch of

road in downtown Greenwich. Parking at dinner time can be a nightmare, and could prevent you from even attempting take-out.

Well, have no fear. You can provide your credit card number when you place your order and then give them a call when you are pulling up to the restaurant. You pull over, and they will run out, hand you your food through your window and let you sign your receipt right in your car. And they always do it with a big smile. In no time you are back home, enjoying a wonderful meal.

Lagniappe Takeaway: Thai Basil understands the importance of access and convenience when take-out is concerned. Here they've turned a bad parking situation into a positive by running out with the food and your receipt. A little something extra indeed.

A WEALTH OF KNOWLEDGE FREELY SHARED

The craft beer world can be a tough one to navigate. What you're looking for regarding taste, price, how the beer complements food, and so forth is a very daunting task that many people are hesitant to undertake. That's where the House of Hops in Raleigh, NC, demonstrates a top level of customer experience. House of Hops employees such as their bartender, Jesse, love to share their knowledge and help consumers find products that will make them happy. Reader, Matt Robinson, had this to offer:

> I'm a beer drinker and find that there's always more to learn. That's what I love about House of Hops. I know that their customer service people on the floor are not paid on commission and genuinely want to help you find products that are going to make you happy. At

no other place in town are there such helpful people readily available to help you at every turn. Even if they don't know the answer to your questions, they'll find the right person in the store to assist you whether it's another team member or even another customer.

Food truck operator, Anthony Reid, often serves at the House of Hops and can also attest to the level of service provided by their team. In Anthony's words:

> When you've got several hundred beers to choose from, the task of selecting just one (or four when you're building a 'to go pack') is so daunting. I appreciate that the House of Hops team goes out of their way to make this process as seamless and convenient as possible. In fact, I trust their judgment so much that I've had their staff build my four pack for me and have never once been disappointed.

CHAPTER 22

#11 - SPECIAL NEEDS

"Be everywhere, do everything,
and never fail to astonish the customer."

—Macy's Motto

THE EXTRAS FOR THOSE WHO REQUIRE A LITTLE EXTRA

The eleventh of the 12 types of Purple Goldfish involves handling "special needs." A little unexpected extra to help your customers who need extra care or attention.

SIGNATURE LAGNIAPPE: RITZ-CARLTON

The Ritz-Carlton hotel chain is notorious for allowing any employee to spend up to $2,000 per day to help make a guest experience right. Is it an old wives' tale though? Here's an excerpt from ritzcarltonleadershipcenter.com:

> We're often asked: 'Can employees at The Ritz-Carlton really spend $2,000 per day per guest?' The answer is, 'yes.' At The Ritz-Carlton, everyone has $2,000/day per guest to make it right or delight, but the money is symbolic. No one is walking around with $2,000 in his or her pocket. However, from day one at your job, you're encouraged and empowered to fix or improve a guest's experience, and you may spend up to $2,000 to do this.

> "Employee empowerment means being able to use my natural ability to create a lasting memory for guests or resolve a guest issue and have the confidence that my company supports me 100% in my effort," explains a senior account executive at The Ritz-Carlton. "Sometimes the most delightful 'wow' moments happen in the blink of an eye. If employees are not empowered and need to cross layers of approval, these moments could be lost forever."

The Ritz strikes again! They never cease their pursuit of perfect execution and a flawless guest experience. Let's look at ten more examples:

JOSHIE THE GIRAFFE

The Ritz might be getting a bit repetitive, but there's a reason for it. They're good at what they do. Chris Hurn, the CEO of Fountain-head Commercial Capital, recently wrote a post on *The Huffington Post* recounting his family's experience at the Ritz-Carlton that blew them away. According to Hurn, here's what happened:

> Recently, my family and I experienced the Ritz-Carlton signature customer service in a way that will be talked about in our family and at my company for many years to come. My wife and two children spent a few days at the Ritz-Carlton on Amelia Island (Florida) while I was in California on business — sadly unable to make the trip with them. Upon returning, we discovered that our son's beloved stuffed giraffe, Joshie, had gone missing. As most parents know, children can become very attached to special blankets, teddy bears and the like. My son is extremely fond of his Joshie and was distraught when faced with the idea of going to sleep without his favorite pal. While trying to put him to bed the first night home, I decided to tell a little white lie.
>
> "Joshie is fine," I said. "He's just taking an extra long vacation at the resort." My son seemed to buy it and was finally able to fall asleep, Joshie-less for the first time in a long while. That very night, the Ritz-Carlton called to tell us they had Joshie. Thankfully, he had been found, no worse for wear, in the laundry and was

handed over to the hotel's Loss Prevention Team. I came clean to the staff about the story I told my son and asked if they would mind taking a picture of Joshie on a lounge chair by the pool to substantiate my fabricated story. The Loss Prevention Team said they'd do it, and I hung up the phone very relieved.

A couple of days went by, and we received a package from the hotel. It was my son's Joshie, along with some Ritz-Carlton-branded "goodies" (a frisbee, football, etc.). Also included in the package was a binder that meticulously documented Joshie's extended stay at the Ritz.

Clearly the Ritz went above and beyond to accommodate the feelings of a child (and had some fun with it while they were at it). Would they have been willing to do this if this had been just another guest that didn't have the clout of Mr. Hurn? Knowing the Ritz's culture, we'd be willing to venture that they would. However, it's important to be aware that gifts and preferential treatment can be misconstrued in a hurry by other customers and the general public in the wake of social media. Ultimately, accommodating needs with a genuine heart and as part of your culture is the key to being successful rather than what your return is going to be.

DISNEY'S GLUTEN FREE OPTIONS

This was taken from a post that Bethann Schaffzin offered on allears.net:

Disneyland was so amazing! First, I emailed Chef Chris Justesen, and he called me directly both before we went (on a Saturday morning) and after we returned (to see how our experience was). For this trip, we had less than one day at the park and chose Disney-land as opposed to California Adventure. Once under the railroad bridge, Chef Chris told me to make a left into City Hall and get the gluten-free list of food destinations within the park.

As we walked around Disneyland, we were able to locate a place to eat just about everywhere. We ended up eating at Rancho del Zocalo in Frontierland (where we happened to be at lunch time) and all of us, kids included, had amazing gluten-free meals. They were reasonable in price, fast, and we had lots of tables to eat at once our food was brought out.

At Chef Chris' suggestion, I asked for the head chef there (a woman whose name I cannot recall at the moment), and she came out, went through our gluten-free options and then asked me to wait for a few minutes, and she brought out the meals herself. We had an excellent time, and no one had so much as a stomach ache! We cannot wait to return. They sincerely care that everyone regardless of limitation have a great and safe time at Disneyland.

Accommodating food allergies is becoming commonplace, but Chef Chris and Disneyland went above and beyond to ensure that Bethann and her family had an incredible experience. The entire Disney staff strove to exceed expectations and ensure that all of their needs were met in a proactive manner rather than being reactive. Good on them!

ALL ABOARD THE ROYAL CARIBBEAN

This post comes to us from cruisecritic.com:

> Each [Royal Caribbean] Freedom-class ship offers 32 accessible cabins -- 16 insides and two suites. One pool and one whirlpool each has a lift so that you can enjoy an at-sea swim. Passengers with hearing and visual impairments can take advantage of sign-language interpreters (on cruises sailing to or from the U.S. and Canada only), portable room kits, assisted-listening devices and closed-captioned televisions, as well as Braille and large-print menus and Braille signs and elevator buttons. You can even utilize the services of an interpreter, as long as you request one no less than 60 days before sailing.

Of course, there are legal ramifications for not sufficiently providing amenities as per the Americans with Disabilities Act. However, Royal Caribbean goes so far and above what is necessary that they leave the competition behind.

DISNEY PREPARES YOUR ROOM JUST RIGHT

This post comes from Margalit Sturm Frances on travelingmom. com:

> On a recent visit to Walt Disney World Resort, we stayed at the Boardwalk Resort and learned firsthand from their head of housekeeping staff how Disney accommodates guests with asthma and allergies. The good news:
>
> • The resort can provide at no extra charge deep dry cleaning with additional shampooing of carpets, upholstery, and drapes as long as the guest notifies the staff in advance.

- Housekeeping can be asked to use only vinegar and baking soda to clean the hotel room during the guest's stay.

- Steaming with hot water of any hard surfaces and bathroom and patio floors.

- Guest room air conditioning filters can be changed.

- Fragrance-free soaps and hypoallergenic pillows are available.

- Bed linens and towels can be sent out and laundered with special hypoallergenic soaps.

Furthermore, the head of housekeeping for the hotel we stayed at mentioned they try to keep a stock of specially washed linens and towels in case they run out unexpectedly. In extreme cases, the hotel can remove the upholstered sofa from the room (if the guest requests it) to minimize allergens.

Though it might not be entirely possible to accommodate every single guest need, Disney goes above and beyond to provide exceptional service. This is made evident by the fact that the housekeeping staff is so in tune with what they can provide that they're able to answer guest questions rather than issuing responses from corporate or general management.

ALLERGY MISCONCEPTIONS

With the explosion of allergies and fad diets, it can be tough to distinguish what an actual medical condition encompasses or whether a guest is just "high maintenance." In our estimation, what's the difference? They're paying a restaurant's bills and if it's reasonable to accommodate the people that allow you to have a roof over your head then you should. As reader, Jessica Harris, explains:

> As a person that has a severe gluten allergy, I appreciate the restaurants that go out of their way to accommodate me. There's a new restaurant that's at Lafayette Village in Raleigh, NC, called Fresh Levant Bistro. The entire restaurant is gluten-free, so I don't have to worry about that and then everything else on their menu is labeled dairy free as well. I would say in general it's just very nice to have the menu clearly marked with which items contain gluten and other allergens.
>
> I especially appreciate it if the restaurant has a separate dedicated fryer so that I can order things like french fries that themselves wouldn't have gluten that when you dip them in the fryer that has also been used to cook things made with flour, then I can't eat them anymore. Chain restaurants that do a superb job of this are Outback Steakhouse, Carrabba's, Panera, Chipotle, and Red Robin.
>
> Also, I use an app that's called "Find me GF" (Gluten Free). I just tap on "search near me" wherever I am, and it pops up a list of restaurants that have gluten-free options.

EMPATHY IS THE SERVICE OF CHOICE

This was taken from Lauren Swick Jordan and was originally posted in *The Washington Post*:

> I am an autism mom. My TJ is 15…[this] is a success story about people who show empathy, kindness, understanding, and acceptance. My family and I live in

a small town. A few miles away from our home is my husband's and my favorite restaurant: Loretta's Fine Italian. We have been eating there for years. It's a small restaurant, and Loretta makes the most delicious food. For years we placed special orders for Christmas Eve take out for our entire family, usually going to pick it up early so we can talk with dear Linda behind the bar as we wait. When TJ's Occupational Therapy Center was fundraising, Loretta chose one night to donate 10 percent of every check to our center.

It's that kind of fantastic, local, family friendly place. And more importantly, we discovered, it is a 'TJ friendly' place. TJ was not having the most flexible of days when we decided to go out to dinner a few weeks ago. We were all sitting around the table when we got our menus.

Sometimes I call ahead to ask if burger and fries, TJ's favorite, are on that night's menu. If it wasn't on the menu, Loretta has been known to go to the market and buy just enough to make just for him. But this night I didn't call ahead. We didn't want TJ always to count on that special treatment. We wanted him to learn to be flexible with limited menu options. When we don't push him, he gets too comfortable, and he doesn't learn. And some of the best advice I had ever heard once was, 'treat him like everyone else – that way he will know what to do to fit into society.' It's an important skill for my boy with autism. For some, however, particularly for a child who is nonverbal, that's not an option.

When TJ saw that there was no burger, he started to get agitated. I said to him, 'Remember, sweetie; you can always order plain buttered noodles. And you get to add your salt!' I got a 'Hrumph' and a furrowed brow. But we were still okay – he was holding it together.

When we placed our order with our lovely waitress, who didn't know us, I asked for TJ's plate to have no garnish. No parsley, no green anything on the plate, nothing but the buttered noodles. She smiled at our quirky order and brought it back to Loretta in the kitchen. TJ sat there fuming. I could tell his anger was building. I asked him to take a deep breath. 'NO!' he yelled. Everyone was looking at us, but that's nothing new. I explained to TJ that he was not allowed to behave like that in public and had to calm himself down. He wasn't happy about it, but he did it. This was not our first rodeo.

A few minutes later the waitress returned. She said, "Loretta said she can make TJ some chicken fingers and fries if he'd rather have that. Would you like that?" "YES! Thank you!" TJ again yelled. But now he was smiling. Beaming. You could sense his relief. Loretta knew it was us. I assume it was the "no parsley or any type of garnish" that gave away our identity. I said to the waitress, "Thank you so much and please tell Loretta that we love her." The waitress returned in a few minutes with some chicken wings, saying "Loretta thought you all might like these while you wait for your dinner."

It is so tough being an autism mom. And to be on the receiving end of such kindness, such understanding almost brought me to tears. Loretta showed us once again that we were safe there, that her place was a place of acceptance and embracing TJ for who he is, good and bad.

I'm not saying that the entire world needs to bend to accommodate our kids and us. What I am saying is that if we are handling our autistic kiddos, as us parents know how to do, a little empathy, kindness, and acceptance goes a long way. Sometimes it is the difference between a hugely positive experience and a negative experience.

I WASN'T GOING ANYWHERE WITHOUT YOU

This example was taken from Christopher Elliott over at elliott. org about a Southwest pilot accommodating a need because of a tragedy:

> Last night, my husband and I got the tragic news that our three-year-old grandson in Denver had been murdered by our daughter's live-in boyfriend. Our grandson is being taken off life support tonight at 9:00 and his parents have opted for organ donation, which will take place immediately. Over 25 people will receive our grandson's gifts tonight and many lives will be saved.

> This morning, after only a couple hours sleep, my husband, Tom, and I began to make all arrangements to get him to Denver to be with our daughter. Tom is currently on business in LA and is flying Southwest. While Tom's employer, Northrop Grumman, made arrangements to get his ticket changed so Tom could get to Tucson today (which he had to do in order not

to spend any extra money), I called Southwest to arrange his flight from Tucson to Denver.

Tom has several free flights with them so I couldn't do it on the website. I was able to get this handled via a ticketing agent on the phone, but Tom found that in LAX that the lines to both check a bag and get through security were exceptional. Tom got to the airport two hours early and was still late getting to his plane. Every step of the way, he's on the verge of tears and trying to get assistance from TSA to get to his plan on time. According to Tom, everyone he talked to couldn't have cared less.

When Tom was done with security, he grabbed his computer bag, shoes, and belt and ran to his terminal in his stocking feet. When Tom finally arrived, the pilot of his plane and the ticketing agent both met him in the terminal and said, "Are you, Mark? We held the plane for you and we're so sorry about the loss of your grandson."

The pilot held the plane that was supposed to take off at 11:50 until 12:02 when my husband got there. As my husband walked down the Jetway with the pilot, he said, "I can't thank you enough for this." The pilot responded with, "They can't go anywhere without me, and I wasn't going anywhere without you. Now relax. We'll get you there. And again, I'm so sorry."

Lagniappe Takeaway: Tragic events and unforeseen circumstances happen. At the end of the day, organizations are made up of people with hearts, minds, and families just like the people that they serve. Don't forget that compassion in a time of need is something that your customers will never forget.

SPECIAL DIETARY ISSUES ARE COVERED

This is an except from a blog post by Hank Davis at the SALT & Pepper Group:

> Faye and I are both pretty big fans of having others do the cooking for us. We eat out a lot, and we also order in quite a bit. We experience food service customer service on a very personal level. Unfortunately for Faye, her food allergies make dining out a sometimes, terrible experience.
>
> Faye cannot have anything dairy, and she cannot even come close to anything from the onion family. She cannot even have something that has touched a grill that has had an onion on it. This makes things tough.
>
> Recently, however, the team at The Rainforest Cafe made it not so tough for her. In fact, they went above and beyond to the point Faye could not wait to get home from her lunch date with a friend to share the great story with me. Here are the five things that happened that blew her away and made her day at The Rainforest Cafe. Here's a summary of what happened:
>
> Faye did not have to volunteer her allergies to the server because the server started off with a great question, "Does anybody have any food allergies we should know about?" She did this with a smile and genuine concern for her guests. Typically, Faye has to initiate an awkward and sometimes uncomfortable conversation about her allergies but not at The Rainforest Cafe. Here are some of the other things that the staff did:
>
> • Faye's server pointed out, with great care and concern, some specific meal options that might match

up with her allergies. She made some excellent suggestions which, in our experience, is rare.

- The server brought out a separate menu that covered many of the allergy concerns that many of their guests have. This was great and made Faye feel pretty special.

- The head chef came out of the kitchen to say hello, introduce himself and see if he could help in any way. He guided Faye through their lunch options, made several specific suggestions and then delivered her meal to her after it was prepared. After the meal, he came back to check to see how she liked it.

- Their team took it as a challenge to delight and please my better half, and that makes me a Raving Fan (shout out to Ken Blanchard) of The Rainforest Cafe. They loved what they were doing, and it made us love their company.

I am planning on going to The Rainforest Cafe again, and I am very thankful for the team that went out of their way to make Faye's day. When she is happy, I am happy, and she was happy. Great work and thank you!

Lagniappe Takeaway: Concerns like food allergies are no small matter to your customer. Go above and beyond to proactively address concerns and demonstrate you care.

EVEN PROTECTORS NEED OUR HELP

In a time where community/police relations have perhaps never been more tumultuous, some companies still find a way to provide a silver lining during such a dark period. The police in Harford County, MD, had just suffered an attack at the hands of the citizens that they had sworn to protect and had lost two of their officers. That's when local restaurant chain, Mission BBQ, swooped in to provide food to the officers, other civil servants, their families, and all of the mourners as they bonded together for support during such difficult times.

According to Mission BBQ's national brand ambassador, Kerry Johnston:

> We didn't need to publicize our actions. That would be self-serving. We just wanted to do the right thing and help take care of people that protect us in their time of need. We also didn't give to get. We all need a little help from time to time...even those that protect and serve. That's exactly why Mission exists.

FOOD ALLERGIES? LET US BOOK A FLIGHT

This final story comes to us from Carmine Gallo over at bloomberg.com about the Ritz-Carlton:

One family was staying at the Ritz-Carlton, Bali, had carried specialized eggs and milk for their son who suffered from food allergies. Upon arrival, they saw that the eggs had broken, and the milk had soured. The Ritz-Carlton manager and dining staff searched the town but could not find the appropriate items. But the executive chef at this particular resort remembered a store in Singapore that sold them. He contacted his mother-in-law and asked that she buy the products and fly to Bali to deliver them, which she agreed to do. Of course, the family was delighted. After an experience like that, do you think this particular family would even consider staying somewhere else?

CHAPTER 23

#12 - HANDLING MISTAKES

"Customers don't expect you to be perfect. They do expect you to fix things when they go wrong."

—Donald Porter

NOBODY IS PERFECT, NOT EVEN A PERFECT STRANGER

The last type of Purple Goldfish will seem like an odd addition to the list. In business, we are conditioned never to admit failure. However, no one is perfect, and we all make mistakes. How you deal with them is the real question. It's important to not only correct the problem but to go above and beyond to make things (more than) right.

The idea of proactively admitting to mistakes is totally unexpected. Admit your wrongdoing, ask the customer what they'd like as amends, and then always exceed their request. This is brilliant on so many levels. First, it is Dale Carnegie-esque...admit when you're wrong and do it emphatically. It takes the steam out of a complaint. Second, it involves the customer as part of the solution. Let them be judge and jury. This speaks volumes about your willingness to make things right. Lastly, you exceed the proposed solution. Within reason, you take the solution and notch it up one or two levels. This gets back to the idea of being totally unexpected.

SIGNATURE LAGNIAPPE: JETBLUE

Inclement weather kept JetBlue Airways passengers trapped on a plane for eight hours in Fort Lauderdale, FL. The flight was supposed to leave for Cancun, Mexico, at 8:15 a.m. but an expected break in the weather never came, resulting in what JetBlue called "unacceptable delays" for its customers. That's a traumatic situation any way that you look at it, especially since the passengers felt that they received no additional information.

JetBlue did the right thing and offered a full refund and a round-trip JetBlue ticket for all of the passengers on the plane. That's a tremendous move on JetBlue's part but what they did next shocked the world. The then-COO, Rob Maruster, of JetBlue took to YouTube and issued a public apology:

> At no point in this weekend was safety ever compromised. But let's face it, you count on us at JetBlue for a lot more -- and we promise a lot more -- and we know we let some of you down over the course of this weekend and for that we are truly sorry.
>
> [JetBlue will] fully participate with the Department of Transportation and cooperating with their investigation into events over the weekend, and we're also going to conduct an internal evaluation so that we can learn from this event because at the end of the day, you deserve better -- and we expect better from our crewmembers and our operation. We can only earn your loyalty and trust one flight at a time, and we ask you to give us a second chance.

JetBlue, as wonderful as they are, cannot control the weather. Not only did JetBlue make up for the purchases that were made but they accepted responsibility for letting their customers down, used the data they garnered to improve their operations, and did not make excuses. Good on JetBlue for going above and beyond to try and make an unfortunate situation into a blessing in disguise.

WHEN YOU'RE WRONG, MAKE IT RIGHT

Reader Brad Rorrer of Fayetteville, NC, had this to say about a recent trip to Mellow Mushroom:

> This past Sunday at the Mellow Mushroom in Myrtle Beach, SC, I got a medium "meaty pizza" and asked for light sauce, but they mistakenly put light sauce on my girlfriend's pizza instead. The manager accepted re-

sponsibility for the mistake, apologized, and comped the pizza. This all happened after I refused a remake of the pizza and insisted that it wasn't a big deal as I'm well aware that these things happen. Without asking, he then proceeded to give me a "to go" soda for the road. I tipped near the price of the pizza ($18) because I was that satisfied.

Lagniappe Takeaway: No one wants to admit that they've made a mistake. Making a mistake is often misconstrued as a weakness and comes from pride, arrogance or fear of a customer not returning. However, those that own up to their failures are seen as more transparent, honest, and trustworthy. Think about it this way, would you rather have an upset customer that tells others about the negative experience or admit your fault to garner a lifetime friend that keeps coming back and spreads the good word about you? The choice seems obvious when you think about it this way.

ALL FEEDBACK IS CREATED EQUAL

131 Main restaurants based out of Cornelius, NC, cares about their guests. Every single one of their Yelp reviews encompasses a full response from 131's corporate management. Here's an example of how 131 made things right on a special day for a couple:

> I'm updating my review from my last. The general manager reached out to me the day I posted my review to go over our poor experiences and he was very apologetic and understanding. He asked my fiancé and I to come back in and give them another try after he addressed the issues. I was very impressed with the customer service. My review was handled quickly and we spoke immediately to try and get our concerns resolved.

Last night, I made a reservation for my fiancé and I to come in and have a dinner to celebrate his birthday. Upon arrival, there was a Happy Birthday balloon waiting for us at the table. Very nice touch! The manager that was on duty introduced himself and also apologized for the previous poor experiences.

Our waiter, Justin, was awesome! We never had an empty drink, his timing was always perfect, and the candle he put in the brownie dessert was also a very nice touch! The steaks were also cooked perfectly the first try this time! Overall, we were extremely satisfied with our most recent experience and will return to enjoy another meal at 131.

131 Main was able to take a negative experience and review and turned the previous mishap into a positive. The last sentence epitomizes what we all aim for when the guest says that they are extremely satisfied and will return for another meal. Thanking all guests for their feedback and rendering the negative situations is common practice at 131. Here's another example of the 131 Main group going above and beyond:

Update: Upon receipt of my email, the manager promptly contacted me (2-3 times) and was insistent (kindly) that he make things right. He did not want that experience to color our long-standing positive view of 131 Main. He made a generous offer to make us whole and gave me his personal cell, should there be any problems in the future. He is everything a manager should be. I really appreciated his kindness and thoughtfulness in handling the mess up.

Lagniappe Takeaway: Many companies will take their respond to overly negative reviews. The difference here is that 131 Main thanks the reviewer for their time, apologizes, and offers a personal phone number to find resolution. What's even more remarkable is that 131 takes the time to thank and make amends for every single review on Yelp. It's clear that 131 Main is vested in guests for the long-term and does everything in its power to make the situation right.

TALK ABOUT OVER-DELIVERING

Reader, Jerry Watterson, had this story to offer from his food blogging community, Jax Restaurant Reviews:

> Our fans, Brian and Lindsay, had a scheduled c-section at Baptist Beaches on Friday. As many of our readers know, with a scheduled c-section, the mother can't eat after midnight the night before. All of Friday Lindsay wasn't allowed to eat anything either, so she had been planning and waiting for the first meal after she had delivered the baby. As for Brian, he was beside Lindsay and would leave to go try to eat food so he wouldn't have to eat in front of her, but he wound up nearly having to fast along with her after a series of unfortunate events involving the hospital cafeteria.
>
> Brian explained, "I was with her all day on Friday, and I had the worst luck with the cafeteria. I tried in the morning to get breakfast, and they stopped serving at 10:00 a.m. and I got there at 11:00 a.m...later that afternoon, I tried to go back to the cafeteria and get lunch at about 2 p.m., and it was closed again. I didn't want to leave her for too long because it was tough with her being in the room after the c-section by herself. The whole Friday was just terrible for me. Finally, it was Saturday, and everything was good, and

Lindsay could eat whatever she wanted. Her request was Maple Street Biscuit Company, which is one of our favorites."

Brian left the hospital and drove over to Maple Street but discovered when he returned to the hospital that Lindsay's food was in the bag, but, unfortunately, Brian's order was missing. Brian was prepared to head back to Maple Street to pick up another order, but Lindsay suggested that they call first and check to see if a bag was left on the counter. Lindsay was directed to the manager, Matt, who quickly looked into the situation and realized that the error had been made by Maple Street. Brian's biscuit simply hadn't made it into the bag.

Whereas most managers at this point would offer a refund or prepare the order for the customer to pick up, Matt immediately offered to go above and beyond. Matt suggested that he would just bring it to the hospital since Brian and Lindsay had been looking forward to this meal. This is where the story gets even better.

Matt and his wife had delivered their baby at Baptist Beaches just a few weeks before, and he understood how stressful the situation was with a newborn, especially with being away from their other child, and being confined to the hospital with a food crisis. Matt prepared Brian and Lindsay's order and arrived at Baptist Beaches in less than 15 minutes.

Brian was walking out to get some air and Matt was already on his way. Brian explained, "He told me again how sorry he was and how he wanted to make sure that everyone was happy. So in addition to bringing our missing order, he put in an extra box of biscuits for all of our visitors and another box of biscuits for the nurses and hospital staff that were working on the unit.

The part that stands out is that I'm not a regular, but he knew me apart from every other customer." Brian laughed and continued, "We go in about once a month to eat so that we don't blow up to 300 pounds. On this day, I was a random customer that walked in and happened not to receive the right order. We didn't push for this customer service; he just knew that this was the way that you treat customers."

CHAPTER 24

LAGNIAPPE CATEGORY: TECHNOLOGY

"The most exciting breakthroughs of the 21st century will not occur because of technology but because of an expanding concept of what it means to be human."

—John Naisbitt

HIGH TECH GUEST EXPERIENCE

Technology is becoming a game changer in marketing. Let's look at some companies that are leveraging the latest technologies to provide a little something extra for customers:

RFID + ICE CREAM = HAPPY GUESTS

This excerpt was taken from a post by *Matrix Product Development*:

> Izzy's Ice Cream Cafe of St. Paul, MN, serves over 150 flavors of handmade ice cream and always keeps 32 flavors in the case on any given day. I talked with Jeff Sommers today, and he is super passionate about his ice cream and providing superior customer service to serve it up.
>
> When customers came to Jeff's store, they wanted to taste their favorite ice cream flavor. Sometimes it was not yet available, and so people would leave feeling disappointed. Some people would purchase a different flavor, but Jeff wanted total customer satisfaction, and he searched for a way to provide it.
>
> Finding a way to let the patron know when their favorite flavor was available and reducing disappointment was a prime concern for Jeff. It was a problem he needed to solve right away. The day he found an RFID technology solution for that problem was the day that revenue increased. Jeff had solved the problem and provided added value.
>
> RFID tags identify each flavor when it is placed in the case ready to serve. The RFID system updates the in-

ventory every three minutes so you can be sure your favorite flavor is there when you have a craving. If you choose to be notified by email, you can sign up and let the system know what flavors you are looking for. There are options to be notified by Twitter updates and Facebook alerts as well. Just sign up for the updates.

The effort Jeff took to find a solution for his customer is remarkable. I find it one of the most unique ways of utilizing RFID tagging technology while bringing top notch customer service to business. When owners like Jeff go out of the way to serve their customer, we believe it's a story worth telling over and over again.

QR CODES AND SQUID INK

A Boston, MA, area restaurant called Taranta has uniquely involved QR Codes in their offering. Chef Jose Duarte uses squid ink to place QR codes on plates featuring fresh locally sourced seafood. Diners can scan the code to visit a site called, "Trace and Trust."[37] It allows you to track where and when your fish was caught.

Lagniappe Takeaway: Talk about a signature extra. This one is signed in squid ink. A clever use a hot button technology to highlight the fact you source fresh seafood from local fishermen.

DO IT ALL FROM THE TABLE

Microsoft PixelSense (formerly known as Surface table computing) is a brilliant concept. Imagine being able to order your food, play games, pay when you please, and interact with the very table that your food and drink sits on. This was a breakthrough in the mid-

---

37. http://traceandtrust.com

2000s, but unfortunately, the $7,000-$12,000 price tag per table deemed the project as more of a novelty rather than a feasible reality. Still, restaurant concepts such as Inamo in London, England, continue to push for technology that helps consumers create the experience of their choosing.

According to Les Shu of digitaltrends.com:

> In this Asian-fusion London restaurant, there are no paper menus. Instead, it's projected onto the table, which you can navigate as you would a tablet. Food is ordered by pressing the virtual buttons on the "e-table," at the customers' leisure. While they wait, diners can watch a video of the kitchen staff preparing their food or pull up info about the local area; they call up the bill at the end of the meal.

> The projection system is even customizable on the fly, allowing the restaurant to change it up for special events. According to the founders, they developed the concept after a dining experience in which they had trouble getting the attention of wait staff. They say the e-table frees up the staff to be more social with diners.

CREATE YOUR TASTE

Tablet ordering technology is becoming more prevalent; that's nothing new. Surprisingly, mega-chain, McDonald's, is one of the larger proponents of technology (though their motives to alleviate labor costs are a major gripe among consumers). One featured piece of technology is the "Create Your Taste" initiative where consumers can order from a kiosk and allows them to design their burgers.

Customers can choose the type of bun, toppings, and dressings as well as "supersizing" their meal without the quintessential, "Would you like fries with that?" line of questioning. According to Valli Herman of the LA Times:

> Touch-screen kiosks that look like giant iPads take customers through the clerk-free customizing process. You can choose a 100% beef patty for $4.99 or a $5.74 burger with 1/3-pound of sirloin. Delivery is promised in eight to 10 minutes. The options include bacon ($1.09 extra) and an assortment of buns, cheeses, toppings, and sauces -- each an upgrade from the usual McDonald's fare.
>
> Buns step up to the artisan roll, tender and buttery, or the sesame seed-topped premium bun, the ciabatta roll or a green leaf lettuce wrap (goodbye iceberg). The cheese isn't the usual industrial yellow lava, but a choice of natural sharp white cheddar, natural pepper jack and, because it's still McDonald's, American.
>
> You can go crazy with toppings, at no additional charge: chili-lime tortilla strips, guacamole, red onion slices, tomatoes, pickles, grilled mushrooms, grilled onions and lettuce leaves. Sauces include the regular ketchup and mustard, but also sweet barbecue, creamy garlic, and peppercorn.
>
> A window populates alongside the order screen as you add burger elements, so that you can, perhaps, reconsider whether you want pepper jack with jalapenos and peppercorn sauce. Other on-screen options allow you to "make it a meal" and add a drink and fries (order a la carte and you'll pay more). Pick up a pager and your food will be delivered to your table in a paper-lined metal basket; fries come in a mini mesh fry basket.

This is a substantially different model that McDonald's has built its empire on but look at all of the lagniappes that McDonald's has included:

1. Free customization of your meal without the worry of human input errors from the cashiers. This process has been simplified by enabling consumers to communicate directly with the kitchen.

2. Free premium ingredients that aren't commonly found on the McDonald's menu.

3. Visualization of what has been ordered so that consumers can put their minds at ease that they'll be receiving exactly what they're ordering.

4. Fast food has typically been deemed as having a cheaper experience complete with calling a guest over a microphone, a plastic tray, paper tray liner, and an assortment of disposable plastic containers. McDonald's has upped their game and ventured into the casual dining approach with pagers and aesthetically pleasing food serving instruments.

NO KEYS NECESSARY

This example comes to us from our good friend, and fellow Goldfish author, Evan Carroll. According to Evan:

> I absolutely love SPG keyless entry at hotels when I'm on the road. In fact, I'll go out of my way to find hotels that offer keyless entry over hotels that don't. That's really just the tip of the iceberg, though. Hotels are really going out of their way to make life more convenient for the event planning community. I can't say

enough great things about Hilton and Ritz-Carlton for example.

Evan presents some interesting points that had us digging where we came across an article explaining how technology is interrupting the event planning and hotel industries concurrently. Brendan Manley over at hotelnewsnow.com, expanded on this idea:

> According to multiple sources, a large part of the engagement process centers on technology, and at multiple stages of the event, from planning and booking to execution and follow-up. From a conceptual standpoint, new and forthcoming technology will aid planners with a suite of tools intended to provide greater control and reporting.
>
> "Technology will continue to be a focus in future meetings," said John Pochopin, director of meetings and special events for The Ritz-Carlton Resorts of Naples, Florida. "From hotels exploring new ways to support meeting planners to meeting planners looking at tools and apps to simplify the planning process, increase attendance, broaden reach and enhance engagement, technology will be a key component in events. To support meeting planners and their programs, hotels will need to be adept at navigating these new technologies."

To this end, Ritz Carlton-launched Chime in 2015, a meeting services app that allows meeting planners to make real-time requests, such as in-room temperature changes, service attention, setup changes and more. The request is then immediately confirmed by an event concierge. Other tech-based services meanwhile are guest-centric, especially those looking to drive engagement and connectivity among convention attendees.

CHAPTER 25

TOP 10 KEY TAKEAWAYS

"Advice is like a tablet of aspirin.
It only works if you actually take it."

—Donald Murphy

L et us count the Top 10 most important takeaways from Purple Goldfish Service Edition (obviously we threw in another for good measure):

#1. THE BIGGEST MYTH IN MARKETING

There is no such thing as meeting expectations. You either exceed them, or you fall short.

#2. CHOOSE WISELY

You can't be all things to all people. You only have two choices as a marketer: Create to spec and face being a commodity or set out to exceed expectations and become remarkable.

#3. SHAREHOLDERS VS. CUSTOMERS?

Business is about creating and keeping customers. Customer experience should be priority number one in your marketing. Stop focusing on the "two in the bush" (prospects) and take care of the "one in your hand" (customers).

#4. VALUE IS THE NEW BLACK

Don't compete on price. Cater to the 70% of consumers that buy based on value. Price is only relative to the value received.

#5. PHELPS COROLLARY TO THE PARETO PRINCIPLE

Traditional marketing is flawed. 80% of your efforts will net 20% of your results. Focus on existing customers instead of the old-school funnel by finding little extras that are tangible, valuable, and talkable.

#6. GROWTH IS DETERMINED BY FIVE FACTORS

The growth of your product or service is similar to that of a goldfish. Growth is determined by five factors: Size of the bowl (Market), # of other goldfish in the bowl (Competition), Quality of the water in the bowl (Business Environment / Economy), First 120 Days of Life (Start-up) and Genetic makeup (Differentiation). Assuming you've already been in business for four months, the only thing you can control is how you differentiate yourself.

#7. PURPLE GOLDFISH STRATEGY

Purple Goldfish Strategy is "differentiation via added value." Finding signature extras that help you stand out, improve customer experience, reduce attrition and drive positive word of mouth.

#8. ACTS OF KINDNESS

Think of lagniappe as an added branded act of kindness. A beacon or sign that shows you care. Marketing via GLUE (giving little unexpected extras). A little something thrown in for good measure.

#9. LAGNIAPPE ECONOMY

There is a middle ground between a Market Economy (quid pro quo) and a Gift Economy (free). A lagniappe economy is where there is an exchange of goods and services for an exact value (market economy), plus a little unexpected extra that is given for good measure (gift economy).

#10. FIVE INGREDIENTS

There are five ingredients or R.U.L.E.S. when creating a Purple Goldfish:

Relevant - The extra should be of value to the recipient.

Unexpected - It should "surprise and delight."

Limited - The extra should be something rare, hard to find or signature to your business.

Expression - It should be a sign that you care

Sticky - It should be memorable and talkable.

#11. VALUE / MAINTENANCE MATRIX

The VM matrix calculates how a brand measures up on two important criteria: value and maintenance. The goal is to be seen as "high value" and "low maintenance" by your customers. There are 12 types of Purple Goldfish based on value and maintenance:

Value	Maintenance
#1 Throw-Ins	#7 Thank You
#2 In the Bag	#8 Added Service
#3 Sampling	#9 Convenience
#4 Impressions	#10 Waiting
#5 Guarantees	#11 Special Needs
#6 Pay It Forward	#12 Handling Mistakes

FINAL THOUGHTS

We hope you have enjoyed the book. We wanted to make five final points about a Purple Goldfish.

YOU CAN'T MAKE CHICKEN SALAD...

You can't make chicken salad out of chicken poop [our apologies for using "poop" as Stan has young boys]. Creating a Purple Goldfish is not a substitute for having a strong product or service. Get the basics right before considering the little unexpected extras.

AUTHENTIC VS. FORCED

A Purple Goldfish is a beacon. A small gift or offering that demonstrates you care. It needs to be done in an authentic way. If it comes across as forced or contrived, you'll eliminate all of the goodwill and negatively impact your product or service.

LIPOSUCTION?

Lagniappe is not a quick fix or for those seeking immediate results. Translation: it's not liposuction. It's equivalent to working out every day. The results gradually build and improve over time.

IT'S A COMMITMENT, NOT A CAMPAIGN

A Purple Goldfish is different than a promotion or limited time offer. It's a feature that becomes embedded into the fabric of your product or service. Add one or a school of goldfish at your convenience, remove them at your peril.

EVERY GREAT JOURNEY BEGINS WITH A SINGLE STEP

Start small when adding a signature extra and add gradually. The best brands are those who boast a whole school of Purple Goldfish.

FURTHER READING

Other books that we highly recommend:

Delivering Happiness by Tony Hsieh

Hug Your Customers by Jack Mitchell

The Next Evolution of Marketing by Bob Gilbreath

Jab, Jab, Jab, Right Hook by Gary Vaynerchuk

The Experience Effect by Jim Joseph

Purple Cow by Seth Godin

It's My Pleasure by Dee Ann Turner

Domino by Linda Ireland

My Story by Stew Leonard

FREE by Chris Anderson

Winning the Customer by Lou Imbriano

99.3 Random Acts of Marketing by Drew McLellan

Five Star Customer Service by Ted Coiné

The End of Business as Usual by Brian Solis

BAM by Barry Moltz

Killing Giants by Stephen Denny

Tipping Point by Malcolm Gladwell

The New Rules of Marketing & PR by David Meerman Scott

The Customer Rules by Lee Cockerell

Be Our Guest by The Disney Institute's Theodore Kinni

Uplifting Service by Ron Kaufman

Return on Relationship by Kathryn Rose and Ted Rubin

ABOUT THE AUTHORS

STAN PHELPS

Stan Phelps is an author, speaker, and experience architect. He believes that today's organizations must focus on meaningful differentiation to win the hearts of both employees and customers.

He is the Founder of Purple Goldfish, a training company that focuses on customer experience and employee engagement solutions. He believes that "differentiation via added value" can be a game changing strategy. For far too long, the overwhelming majority of marketing has fixated on the eyes and ears of the prospect. Not enough has been focused on creating experiences for current customers that drive referrals. Great customer experience is about being so remarkable that people can't help but talk about you. That if you absolutely delight someone – they will not only come back, but they'll bring their friends.

Before Purple Goldfish, Stan had a twenty-year career in marketing included leadership positions at IMG, adidas, PGA Exhibitions, and Synergy. At Synergy, he worked on award-winning experiential programs for top brands such as KFC, Wachovia, NASCAR, Starbucks, and M&M's.

Stan is the author of four books and a Forbes contributor. His writing is syndicated on top sites such as Customer Think and Business 2 Community. He has spoken at over 100 events in the US, Canada, UK, France, Sweden, The Netherlands, Russia, Peru, Israel, Bahrain, and Australia.

Stan received a BS in Marketing and Human Resources from Marist College, a JD/MBA from Villanova University, and a certificate for Achieving Breakthrough Service from Harvard Business School. He is a Certified Net Promoter Associate and has taught as an adjunct professor of marketing at NYU and Manhattanville College. He is the President of the Triangle AMA, a chapter of the American Marketing Association.

Stan lives in Cary, NC with his wife, Jennifer, and two boys, Thomas and James.

stan@purplegoldfish.com

BROOKS BRIZ

Brooks Briz is an accomplished restaurateur, writer, and speaker. Brooks believes that today's organizations have no choice but to be deliberate in their overall guest experience including their acquisition, retention, and referral strategies. Brooks also believes that relationships must be premeditated and based on mutual values in order to attract and retain the right stakeholders: team members, guests, partners, community, and investors.

Before Brooks became a restaurateur, he accrued over ten years of experience working in multi-unit consulting, operational management, and all facets of front-of-house and back-of-house restaurant positions. Brooks has consulted from single unit restaurants to some of the largest restaurant chains in the world. He has also helped started multiple restaurant brands from scratch and most recently served as the chief marketing officer at Kamado Grille restaurants based in Raleigh, NC.

Brooks is the author of six books including a Dummies social media title (published by Wiley). His next book, Restaurant 3.0, explores the convergence of five pillars for restaurants to remain relevant in

2016 and moving forward: culture, information technology, hospitality, leadership, and the customer experience.

Brooks received a BS/BA in Marketing and Economics from Salisbury University as well as his MBA. Brooks lives in Raleigh, NC, with his pet ball python, Samsonite.

heybrooks@brooksbriz.com

MORE BOOKS IN THE PURPLE GOLDFISH SERIES

WHAT'S YOUR PURPLE GOLDFISH? – 12 WAYS TO WIN CUSTOMERS AND INFLUENCE WORD OF MOUTH.

The book is based on the Purple Goldfish Project, a crowdsourcing effort that collected over 1,001 examples of signature added value. The book draws inspiration from the concept of lagniappe, providing twelve practical strategies for winning the hearts of customers and influencing positive word of mouth.

WHAT'S YOUR GREEN GOLDFISH? – BEYOND DOLLARS: 15 WAYS TO DRIVE EMPLOYEE ENGAGEMENT AND REINFORCE CULTURE.

Green Goldfish examines the importance of employee engagement in today's workplace. The book showcases fifteen ways to increase employee engagement. Signature ways beyond compensation to reinforce the culture of an organization.

WHAT'S YOUR GOLDEN GOLDFISH? – THE VITAL FEW: ALL CUSTOMERS AND EMPLOYEES ARE NOT CREATED EQUAL.

Golden Goldfish examines the importance of your Top 20 percent of customers and employees. The book showcases nine ways to increase to drive loyalty and retention with these two critical groups.

BLUE GOLDFISH: USING TECHNOLOGY, DATA, AND ANALYTICS TO DRIVE BOTH PROFITS AND PROPHETS

A Blue Goldfish occurs when a business leverages technology, data, and analytics to do a "little something extra" to improve the experience for the customer. The book is based on a collection of over 300 case studies. It examines the three R's: Relationship, Responsiveness, and Readiness. *Blue Goldfish* also uncovers eight different ways to turn insights into action.

COMING SOON: RED GOLDFISH

Purpose is changing the way we work and how customers choose business partners. By 2020, there will no longer be a distinction between for profit and non-profit companies. Businesses will either be seen as "for purpose" or "not for purpose." In the forthcoming book *Red Goldfish*, Stan Phelps and Graeme Newell will share lessons from the Red Goldfish Project, revealing the five ways businesses can embrace purpose.

For more information on the Purple Goldfish Series, please visit PurpleGoldfish.com.

39804163R00136

Made in the USA
San Bernardino, CA
03 October 2016